POKER: THE REAL DEAL

BY PHIL GORDON AND JONATHAN GROTENSTEIN

S|S|E

SIMON SPOTLIGHT ENTERTAINMENT
New York London Toronto Sydney
An imprint of Simon & Schuster
1230 Avenue of the Americas, New York, New York 10020
Text copyright © 2004 by Phil Gordon and Jonathan Grotenstein
All rights reserved, including the right of reproduction in whole
or in part in any form.
SIMON SPOTLIGHT ENTERTAINMENT
and related logo are trademarks of Simon & Schuster, Inc.
Design and Typography: Interrobang Design Studio
Manufactured in the United States of America
The original version of this book is cataloged with the Library of Congress.
ISBN-13: 978-1-4169-6136-9
ISBN-10: 1-4169-6136-4

THE BASICS

Poker became the national card game of the United States because it so well suits the American temperament. It is a game for the individual. Each player is on his own, the master of his fate.... It fits any situation, whether it is a serious game among experts or a hilarious game for the entertainment of family and friends who just want to have a good time.... Poker is easy to learn, and once learned is never forgotten. And the cost of the equipment is inconsiderable; there is no more economical form of recreation than card-playing.

—ALBERT H. MOREHEAD,
The Complete Guide to Winning Poker

You've immersed yourself in the history of poker, maybe you've rented some of the movies. You don't know it yet, but you've developed an itch that only poker can scratch. As the old joke goes, "Sex is good, but poker lasts longer."

THE CARDS

Obviously, the first thing you'll need to embark on your poker career is a deck of cards. Many professional poker players carry one with them at all times. They're especially useful on airplanes or in restaurants, where you'll always be able to deal a hand of "negotiation poker" or "Lenny's Delight" . . . but we'll get to that later.

While you can play with any fifty-two-card deck, a stickler for details will tell you that standard poker cards are $3\frac{1}{2}$" x $2\frac{1}{2}$". Fortunately, unless you grew up in a house with a bridge *parlor*, poker cards are what you have always considered to be a normal deck. (The deck used for bridge, a game where you have to hold a lot of cards at once, is a little narrower.)

The first choice is one that you've probably had to make before: paper or plastic.

Paper cards are relatively inexpensive, but they start to deteriorate after a few sessions. Bee and Bicycle are the most common brands used by casinos and cardrooms, but if you do some digging, you'll discover all kinds of interesting alternatives, like Mohawks, Steamboats, and Torpedoes.

Plastic cards, which are used in many casinos, are a lot more durable, a little bit easier to shuffle, and they can even be washed with soap and water. They're also about five times more expensive than paper cards, but the companies that make them (Kem and Royal, to name two) promise that they'll last long enough to pay for themselves many times over.

If you're looking to depart from the classic tradition,

there are plenty of manufacturers and novelty shops that will let you design your own cards, from a simple monogram on the back to the faces of your family members on the front.

THE DONDORF DECK

Today's playing cards are mass-produced in fairly generic styles, but it hasn't always been this way. One notable exception was the Dondorf Company, a German family of artisans who, from 1833 to 1933, unveiled series after series of unique designs that many collectors claim were the most beautiful cards ever produced.

To celebrate the company's 100th anniversary, the Dondorfs designed what would be their most lavish and intricate deck to date, produced in the most limited of limited editions and handed out at the centennial festivities. The elaborate design on the backs of the cards demanded sixteen separate color printings; the intricately detailed fronts required twelve more of their own.

The anniversary deck proved to be the end of the Dondorfs. The cost of printing the cards, coupled with the economic depression that had swept the world, drove the proud company into bankruptcy.

While idealism may have killed the artist, the

legacy lives on today: Altenburger-Stralsunder, the company that purchased the remains of the Dondorf operation, continues to make reproductions of many Dondorf designs.

THE LANGUAGE OF BETTING

Before you can start playing, you have to learn the language of betting. Fortunately, there aren't that many words. Every time the action gets to you, you're going to have to do one of five things:

1. **Fold**. Lay your hand down and exit the pot.
2. **Call**. Match the bet that is in front of you. If there is no bet in front of you, you can . . .
3. **Check** (pass or "no bet," if you're British) the action to the next player,
4. **Bet** (if you're the first person to act), or
5. **Raise** someone else's bet.

Knowing those five words will allow you to communicate with poker players all over the world. Feel the power coursing through your veins.

THE DEAL

For those new to Texas Hold'em, it is probably the easiest form of widow poker to learn, "widow" being a somewhat more colorful term for cards dealt in the center of the table that are shared by each of the players. In hold'em, these community cards—five in all—are called the **board.**

Almost every hold'em game played today incorporates what's called a **blind.** Some use a single blind—a mandatory bet posted by the player just to the left of the dealer—but most incorporate a **big blind** (whatever the table rules determine to be a full bet) and a **small blind** (a fraction of that full bet).

Blinds, like their cousin the **ante**, are designed to encourage action. Think about it this way: Without blinds, the first person to throw in a bet would be risking money to win nothing. These aren't appealing odds to a thinking poker player, who wouldn't open the betting without the strongest of hands. The blinds, however, create instant **pot odds** (a concept we'll get into later), giving a player the chance to win something more than what he or she has wagered.

Once the blinds have been posted, play proceeds as follows:

1. Two cards—the **hole cards**—are dealt facedown to each player.
2. The player sitting to the left of the big blind—the position known as under the gun—has the option to call or raise the blind. Betting continues around the table. You have to pay to play: If you don't call a bet (or any subsequent raises), you have to fold.

3. Once the round of betting has been completed, a group of three cards—better known as the **flop**—is laid faceup on the table.

4. Another round of betting is initiated by the player sitting closest to the left of the dealer (often the small blind). Unlike the opening round, you don't have to bet—you can opt to check instead. If someone else bets, however, you're going to have to call or raise to stay in.

5. Another community card, also known as **fourth street** or the **turn**, is dealt, followed by another round of betting, once again initiated by the person sitting closest to the dealer's left who still happens to be in the pot.

6. A final community card, **fifth street** or the **river**, is placed on the table. A final round of betting ensues.

7. Showdown. The best hand wins.

8. The deal moves to the left and the cycle repeats.

SHOWDOWNS

If you're reading this book, you probably already know all about showdowns. In the unlikely event that you don't, or you just don't remember whether a straight flush beats a full house, you may want to commit the following to memory:

Royal Flush
A straight, ace to ten, all of the same suit.

Ex.

Straight Flush

Any five consecutive cards of the same suit.

Ex. 2♣ 3♣ 4♣ 5♣ 6♣

Four of a Kind

Exactly what you'd think it would be. Also called a **case**.

Ex. K♠ K♣ K♥ K♦ 4♦

Full House

Three of a kind, plus two of a kind. This hand would be "fours full of threes." Also called a **boat**.

Ex. 4♦ 4♥ 4♣ 3♦ 3♠

Flush

Any five cards of the same suit. The hand below is a queen-high flush, which would lose to a king-high flush, etc. If the highest card is a community card, ties get broken by the second card, third card, etc.

Ex. Q♥ 10♥ 7♥ 4♥ 2♥

Straight

Five consecutive cards of any suit.

Ex. 10♣ 9♥ 8♣ 7♦ 6♦

Three of a Kind

Also called **trips** or a **set**.

Ex. 6♣ 6♥ 6♦ A 8♦

Two Pair

The example below would be "queens and jacks" or "queens over jacks."

Ex. Q♥ Q♦ J♥ J♣ 3 ♥

One Pair

If your two matching cards are both hidden, you have a **pocket pair**.

Ex. A♠ A♥ K♥ 9♦ 4♣ ♣

High Cards

If no one has a hand, the highest card (or cards) win(s).

Ex. A♠ 9♦ 8♣ 7♦ 2 ♣

beats A♠ 8♣ 7♦ 3♦ 2 ♦

LIMITS FOR BEGINNERS

Now that you know how to bet, let's talk for a minute about *how much* you can bet.

"Ring" games, a fancy term for a normal poker game (as opposed to a tournament), come in three basic flavors: **structured limit**, **no-limit**, and **pot-limit**.

If you're new to the game, you're going to want to stick to a structured limit game, that is, one where the size of the bet is fixed on each street. For example, in a "$5/10" hold'em game, the bets (or raises) are made in increments of $5 before and just after the flop—the **small bet**—but increase to units of $10 on the turn and the river—the **big bet**.

A no-limit game is exactly what the name suggests, a game in which there's no limit to the amount that you can bet at any time. (Note that there is often a minimum size for each bet or raise.) Many online and casino no-limit games have a maximum buy-in, such as $50 or $500. This helps to prevent one player from steamrolling over everyone else simply by virtue of starting with a much larger **stack** of chips. Any chips that you earn above and beyond the buy-in, however, can be used to bully new players at will.

Pot-limit is a sophisticated hybrid of the two in which you can make a maximum bet at any time of up to the amount of money that is currently in the pot. It's a lot trickier than it sounds. Suffice to say here that there's a galaxy of difference between a $5/10 limit hold'em game (where pots can get into the low hundreds) and a $5/10 pot-limit game (where those same pots can climb into the thousands).

♥ ♦ ♣ ♠ ♥ ♦ ♣ ♠ ♥ ♦ ♣ ♠ ♥ ♦ ♣ ♠ ♥ ♦ ♣ ♠ ♥ ♦ ♣ ♠

YOUR DEFINING MOMENT

You're out at the local Hallmark store picking up a Get Well Soon card for your sick grandmother. After taking a wrong turn at the fake Lladro figurines, you find yourself smack dab in front of a display of Kem Cards. The $19.99 price tag seems a bit high for a couple of cut-up sheets of plastic, but you just won $25 on a scratch-off lottery ticket. You decide to take the plunge. Your life will never be the same.

When you get home, you cut the cellophane and take the cards out of the box. You begin to shuffle. You're a natural. Getting a little cocky, you go for "the bridge." The cards slip from your hands, flying wildly around the room.

What happens next is a miracle—as the cards land on the floor, most of them group together in clusters of seven. Recognizing this as a training opportunity courtesy of the poker gods, you organize each cluster of cards into the best possible five-card hand . . .

Cluster #1:

| 2♥ | 7♥ | 3♦ | 3♣ | A♦ | 4♥ | 5♣ |

Cluster #2:

| 2♣ | 2♦ | 2♠ | 9♣ | 9♥ | 5♥ | 5♠ |

Cluster #3:

| 4♠ | 6♠ | A♠ | Q♦ | 10♠ | K♥ | J♦ |

Cluster #4:

| J♥ | 9♦ | 10♣ | J♠ | 8♥ | J♦ | 7♣ |

Cluster #5:

| 3♠ | 3♥ | A♦ | 4♦ | 6♥ | 6♣ | 4♣ |

Cluster #6:

| Q♦ | K♠ | K♦ | Q♣ | Q♥ | 8♣ | K♠ |

Cluster #7:

| 10♦ | 5♦ | A♦ | 7♦ | 6♦ | 9♠ | 8♦ |

Extra Credit:

Which of the hands above could be improved by replacing one of its cards with one of the three leftover cards?

| 7♠ | 8♠ | 10♥ |

♥ ♦ ♣ ♠ ♥ ♦ ♣ ♠ ♥ ♦ ♣ ♠ ♥ ♦ ♣ ♠ ♥ ♦ ♣ ♠

THE ANSWERS

Cluster #1:

Straight (an ace-to-five straight is called a "bicycle")

| A ♦ | 2 ♥ | 3 ♦ | 4 ♣ | 5 ♣ |

Cluster #2:

Full House ("twos full of nines")

| 2 ♣ | 2 ♦ | 2 ♠ | 9 ♣ | 9 ♥ |

Cluster #3:

Queen-High Flush

| Q ♠ | J ♠ | 10 ♠ | 6 ♠ | 4 ♠ |

Cluster #4:

Jack-High Straight

| 7 ♣ | 8 ♠ | 9 ♦ | 10 ♣ | J ♥ |

Cluster #5:

Two Pair ("sixes over fours with an ace **kicker**")

| 6 ♥ | 6 ♣ | 4 ♦ | 4 ♣ | A |

Cluster #6:

Full House ("kings full of queens")

| Q ♦ | K ♣ | K ♦ | K ♠ | Q ♥ |

Cluster #7:

Ace-High Flush (but *almost* a Straight Flush)

| A ♦ | 10 ♦ | 8 ♦ | 7 ♦ | 6 ♦ |

Extra Credit:

Cluster #4—replace the 9 ♦ with any of the discards to make a Full House. Or Cluster #3—replace the 6 ♠ or 4 ♠ with the 7 ♠ or 8 ♠ to get a higher flush.

THE FIRST DAY OF SCHOOL

You'll practice your grip on the cards; what's important is that you've developed a grip on the basics. You're ready to play the damn game.

Only you don't want to just play. You want to win.

As you sit at the lunch counter poring over the pages of this book, a fellow diner shoots you a cynical look. "What's the point of reading a book about poker? I thought it was all about luck."

Well, he's right. A poker player has to be lucky—in the same way that Warren Buffet gets lucky playing the stock market year after year.

When played "correctly"—with the intention of winning

money—poker is a lot like value investing. You bet heavily on hands that you have a better than average chance of winning, and you minimize your outlay for those that you don't.

So while poker does ultimately come down to luck, there's absolutely nothing to prevent an educated player from taking advantage of fortune's ups and downs.

The concepts that follow represent the cornerstone of a poker education, beginning with a few more myths that have to be dispelled.

"ANY TWO CARDS CAN WIN!"

Getting dealt a seven and a deuce of different suits—a hand we'll call 7-2 offsuit, or 7-2o for short—might not seem as glamorous as "waking up" with pocket aces. But if the flop comes 7-7-2, you are looking at a **monster**. You've got to play everything, because you never know what the flop will bring. Any two cards can win!

You'll hear this cry often, especially at poker's lower limits. And here's a little secret . . . it's true!

Well, it's technically true, anyway. A much deeper truth is this: While any two cards can win, some combinations win a lot more often than others.

Go back to the example above. The player holding 7-2o needs a 7 or a 2 to make a pair. Neither of those pairs alone would be good enough to beat a hand like a pair of aces; to win, this player is actually going to have to make at least two pair or three of a kind while hoping the aces don't improve.

The player with pocket aces, on the other hand, doesn't

need to improve at all. All he or she has to hope for is that the player with 7-2o doesn't get lucky.

Make that *really* lucky—in a **heads-up** showdown, pocket aces will make the better hand around 88 percent of the time.*

Poker, especially limit poker, is a game of **expected value**. You win money by betting in situations in which you have a positive expected value, and holding on to it when your expected value is negative.

This may sound like a tricky mathematical concept, but it's actually pretty easy. Let's say that you find yourself in an A-A vs. 7-2o showdown one hundred times. To keep it simple, let's say each player bets $5 each time, for a total of $10 in each pot. Over the course of a hundred hands, each of you will have wagered $500 ($5 x 100 hands), or $1,000 total.

The person with A-A can expect to win 88 percent of the time, or 88 of the 100 times. Each pot is $10, so the person with **wired** aces should win around $880. That's a $380 profit: $880 in winnings minus the $500 you've contributed to the hundred pots. In other words, the aces have a very healthy positive expected value. The player with 7-2o, on the other hand, will only win the remaining 12 out of 100 times, raking in a total of $120. Subtract the $500 invested, and this player is looking at a $380 *loss*, an unseemly negative expected value.

The first secret to winning hold'em, therefore, is to learn which hands have positive expected value. This is a skill called **hand selection**.

* Don't worry about how those odds were calculated—it's damn near impossible to figure out without a "poker calculator." You can find poker calculators on the Web; *Cardplayer* magazine offers a particularly good one at *www.cardplayer.com*.

SOME PERCENTAGES

If you have a pocket pair, you'll flop a set about 12 percent of the time.

If you have A-K, you'll flop at least a pair about 37 percent of the time.

If you have two suited cards, you will flop four cards to a flush about 11 percent of the time.

What makes some hands better than others? Taking a lesson from the example, it's clear that pocket pairs, especially big ones, can be very powerful, as they can win without any extra help from the board. When they do match up with the community cards, they'll make brawny hands like sets and full houses. Higher cards are better than lower ones, as they make bigger hands (with bigger kickers). Cards that are of the same suit—a condition we'll call **suited**—have a better chance of making flushes, while consecutive (or near-consecutive) cards—**connectors**—are more likely to make straights. **Suited connectors** are even better, increasing your odds of making a straight, flush or, on rare occasions, a straight flush. Hands that incorporate both hole cards are generally stronger than hands that use only one, as you're less likely to end up in a tie with an opponent, forcing you to split the pot.

HOLD'EM POKER FOR ADVANCED PLAYERS
by David Sklansky and Mason Malmuth

No poker library would be complete without this book, arguably the most powerful text ever written on Texas Hold'em.

It can be an infuriating book to read. Sklansky (who you should recognize as one of the contributors to *Super/System*) and Malmuth are men of mathematics, not, as they readily admit, masters of clear communication. Even if you're hip to scientific language, the book offers so much so fast that it can take multiple readings to digest some of the concepts within.

But oh, what concepts they are. During the course of your poker career, you will frequently make astounding discoveries at the table—a novel new way, perhaps, to handle a particular situation—only to find out later that Sklansky and Malmuth had addressed that very situation in a seemingly tossed-off line you managed to completely overlook during your previous readings.

The book's greatest claim to fame might be found in its first few pages, a chart ranking what Sklansky and Malmuth have determined to be the seventy or so "playable" hold'em hands. Pocket aces sit mightily at the top of the heap, while the much humbler 10-8o dwells in the cellar. (That 7-2o of the earlier example—the absolute worst hand in hold'em as it can't use both cards to make a straight or a flush—doesn't make the cut.)

Sklansky and Malmuth break these hands down into eight separate groups, from best to worst, reprinted here with the permission of the authors and Two Plus Two Publishing LLC:

Group 1: A-A, K-K, Q-Q, J-J, A-Ks*

Group 2: 10-10, A-Qs, A-Js, K-Qs, A-K

Group 3: 9-9, J-10s, Q-Js, K-Js, A-10s, A-Q

Group 4: 10-9s, K-Q, 8-8, Q-10s, 9-8s, J-9s, A-J, K-10s

Group 5: 7-7, 8-7s, Q-9s, 10-8s, K-J, Q-J, J-10, 7-6s, 9-7s, A-xs, 6-5s

Group 6: 6-6, A-10, 5-5, 8-6s, K-10, Q-10, 5-4s, K-9s, J-8s, 7-5s

Group 7: 4-4, J-9, 6-4s, 10-9, 5-3s, 3-3, 9-8, 4-3s, 2-2, K-xs, 10-7s, Q-8s

Group 8: 8-7, A-9, Q-9, 7-6, 4-2s, 3-2s, 9-6s, 8-5s, J-8, J-7s, 6-5, 5-4, 7-4s, K-9, 10-8

These rankings have engendered some controversy over the years as critics, often armed with computer simulations, quibble over the values assigned to certain hands. Anyone who regularly watches the professional game will see hands played that, somehow, Sklansky and Malmuth managed to overlook, such as the 10-2 that Doyle Brunson used to win both of his World Series bracelets.

There's no denying, however, that this is *the* list by which all others are judged. Every serious poker player has committed these hand rankings to memory.

---

* The "s" signifies two cards of the same suit, while "x" indicates any small card. "A-xs," therefore, means an ace with a smaller card of the same suit.

"NEVER DRAW FOR AN INSIDE STRAIGHT"

Everybody knows that drawing to an inside straight is a sucker's play. There's only one card in the deck (well, four cards, to be precise) that can help you.

Or can they?

In most cases, if you're going to draw at a straight, you should at least be **open-ended**—

You   The Board

(any ace or nine will save you)

—or on a **double belly-buster**—

You   The Board

(a king or a nine will do)

Draws—those hands where you decide to stick around for another bet or two in the hopes of improving—are the reason so many poker players suffer from something akin to bipolar disorder. Spike a big draw on the river, and you'll smile as you rake in a very big pot. Chase and miss, however, and you've paid an expensive price for a whole lot of misery.

So when is it right to draw? Same as when it's correct to play a hand: when the expected value of betting that hand is positive. What's different, however, is that you don't need a poker calculator to do the computations. A third-grade math education will do.

Let's use a simple coin flip as an example. You have a

50 percent chance of flipping heads. But what are the odds *against* flipping heads? Well, if you flip that coin one hundred times, the results should be somewhere in the neighborhood of fifty heads and fifty tails. Your odds against flipping heads are 50 to 50, or 1-to-1.

Gamblers like odds, because they quickly indicate whether or not a wager has a positive expectation. If the odds against flipping heads are 1-to-1, you'd want to be getting (at least) odds of 1-to-1 on your money, or a dollar paid for a dollar risked. After 100 flips of the coin, you will have made $50 for the times you made heads, but you'll have lost $50 on those instances when the coin came up tails. A break-even proposition.

Now let's say that your grandmother, after one martini too many, offers you 2-to-1 odds on that same coin flip. In other words, she'll pay you $2 every time you win, but only take $1 each time you lose. After 100 flips of the coin, you'll still have forked over $50 for all of the tails, but you'll have won $100 for the heads. You should be able to take the hapless matron for somewhere in the neighborhood of $50.

This concept makes its way into poker in the form of pot odds. If there's $40 in the pot, and a $10 bet in front of you, the pot is laying you odds of $40 to $10, or 4-to-1. As you might expect, you are getting the correct pot odds to call a bet as long as your odds of making the best hand are 4-to-1 or better.

Okay, this part is a little tricky: You're getting "4-to-1 odds" on your draw when you have a hand that will miss four times for every one time that it hits. In other words, a hand with 4-to-1 odds is a hand that you'll hit once in every *five* tries.

Think about it in terms of the pot. If there's $40 in the pot, and it's costing you $10 to call, how often do you need to succeed? You can miss four times—that will cost you $40—but if you hit it the fifth time, you'll win the $40 pot (plus the $10 you risked) and come out even.

Let this settle in for a minute: It's the toughest mathematical concept you'll have to master in order to be a winning poker player. When you talk about a hand that's getting 4-to-1 odds on a draw, what you are really saying is that you are going to complete that draw one time in five, or 20 percent of the time.

So how do you know if your hand will win 20 percent of the time? You start by determining which cards can help you make your hand. Poker players call these **outs**.

Go back to the two straight draws at the beginning of this section. In each case, two different cards would make your hand. Each of those cards comes in four different suits, making eight cards in all that can help you. In other words, you have eight outs to your straight.

Okay, now what? Well, that depends on how much you like math. If you're well versed in the laws of statistical probability, feel free to run through four or so steps of calculation required to determine an accurate answer. If you're just looking for a quick estimate—which is all you'll need in most cases—use the **rule of four**: Multiply the number of outs by four, and you'll have a rough approximation of your chances of completing your hand with two cards (the turn and the river) to come. In this case, with eight outs, you have about a 32 percent chance of making your hand.

Now we have to figure out the odds. If you're going to win this scenario 32 percent of the time (32/100, or about once in every three times), then you are going to lose 68 percent of the time (about two out of every three times). Your odds of making the straight, therefore, are approximately 2-to-1 against.

So should you chase your eight-outer? Yes, as long as the pot contains $2 for every $1 you have to wager.

One final word on odds: The rule of four is used to calculate the odds of making your hand with *two* cards to come, the turn and the river. You may have noticed an implication here: You may have to call not just one, but *two* bets, in order to see a river card. Doesn't this screw up our analysis of pot odds?

The simple answer—yes, it does. Do you have to worry about it? Not very often, thanks to a concept called **implied pot odds**. This is basically a fancy way of saying that, before the hand is over, the pot is going to grow even larger. In most cases, if you're getting the right odds to pay to see the turn card, you're going to be getting the right odds to fork over a second bet to see the river. If you ever find yourself doubting the wisdom of making a particular bet, you can multiply your number of outs by *two* instead of four, giving you a rough approximation of your chances of making the hand with one card to come instead of two.

In truth, this is a gross oversimplification of implied pot odds. For a far more thorough treatment, you'd do well to read *The Theory of Poker* (see below).

The good news—this is the last math lesson in the book. As a reward for getting through it, here's a useful tip:

The larger the pot, the more inclined you should be to win it as quickly as possible.

The reasoning behind this is simple once you've grasped the concept of pot odds. Decent-sized pots generally provide correct odds for your opponents to call bets with their open-ended straights or four-card flushes. Once a pot gets large, however, your opponents will have the right odds to draw for all kinds of hands. Eleven-to-one odds are enough to make it okay to break that cardinal rule and draw for the inside straight. A huge pot—capped before the flop—may give your opponents good reason to draw with unimproved pocket pairs (looking for the two outs that will make them a set) or even **backdoor flushes**.

Nip these speculators in their respective buds by taking down those pots before the odds get crazy enough for them to start acting crazy. We'll get to the tools that will help you accomplish this in the next section.

THE THEORY OF POKER

by David Sklansky

The guy didn't earn the nickname "Einstein" for nothing. No one has contributed more to the study of the scientific principles governing poker than David Sklansky.

The Theory of Poker is his masterpiece. He covers, from the ground up, everything you need to know about the mathematics of odds, implied odds, check-raising, even bluffing. Perhaps his most brilliant stroke is the Fundamental Theorem of Poker:

Every time you play a hand differently from the way you would have played it if you could see all your opponents' cards, they gain; and every time you play your hand the same way you would have played it if you could see all their cards, they lose. Conversely, every time opponents play their hands differently from the way they would have if they could see all your cards, you gain; and every time they play their hands the same way they would have played if they could see all your cards, you lose.

Okay, poetry it's not. But powerful, powerful stuff. *The Theory of Poker* belongs on every poker player's bookshelf.

"THE DEAL IS OF NO SPECIAL VALUE"

The next myth to be dispelled is from a pamphlet on poker, written in the late nineteenth century by General Robert Schenck, the American ambassador to England, who intended to teach the finer points of the game to a British duchess. Whatever other virtues General Schenck might have possessed, he was dead wrong about the value of being the dealer.

In the example presented earlier, pocket aces worked very effectively in a heads-up battle against one other player. Hold'em, however, is a game that's usually dealt nine- or ten-handed. Most of the time—especially early in your poker career—you will be up against more than one player. Where you act in relation to these other players— your **position**—is extremely important. And as you might remember from the previous chapter, the player seated in the dealer position gets to act last during every round of betting from the flop on.

Why is this so important? For the simple reason that you get to see what everyone else is up to before having to commit any money yourself. If there's a lot of raising or re-raising in front of you, it might be wise to fold your hand. If everyone checks to you, a bluff at the pot might be in order.

Relative position is a critical factor in determining just how strong a hand you are holding. Some hands that might initially seem valuable are actually very difficult to play if you have to decide whether to check, bet, or fold before a large field of other players who are set to act.

Before the flop, your position at the table is usually broken down into four basic categories:

1. **Early Position** (EP). The two or three players seated directly to the left of the blinds have to decide before anyone else does whether or not to enter—or raise—the pot. There could be a lot of scary hands out there. (The player in first position is said to be under the gun for this very reason.) It's usually wise, therefore, to limit yourself to the stronger hands of the hold'em spectrum.

2. **Middle Position** (MP). The three or four players in the middle have an easier time of it. They get to see what the EPs do before the flop, and won't have to make any decisions after the flop until the blinds and EPs have acted. It's a luxury that allows you to play a relatively wider selection of hands. If no one has entered the pot

before you, you can think about raising with some of the hands you might have thrown away from early position. And if an EP has already raised, you can safely fold some of your marginal holdings.

3. **Late Position** (LP). This is the area some poker players like to call "the office," as it's the best place from which to do your work at the table. The crown jewel of late position is the **button**, or the dealer's seat. As the button, you not only get to act last on every round of betting after the flop, but if no one has entered the pot before you, you can try to **steal the blinds**, raising with a hand that wouldn't ordinarily be worth two bets in the hopes of scaring the blinds into folding.

4. The **Small** and **Big Blinds** (SB & BB). These may be the trickiest positions to play well in Texas Hold'em. It might seem like a great seat before the flop: Not only do you get to act last, but you get to enter the pot at a discount (since you've already posted a bet or a fraction of a bet), giving you the right odds to play many weaker-than-usual hands. After the flop, however, the blinds are obligated to act first on every round, making it extremely dangerous to play those weaker hands.

As a basic rule of thumb, you generally don't want to play anything from early position worse than what Sklansky and Malmuth call a Group 4. Playing hands from Group 5 or 6 is usually okay from middle position. Hands from Group 7 and 8 are best played, if at all, from late position or for a fractional bet from the blinds.

This rule of thumb, however, greatly depends on how your opponents play. Against very aggressive competition, you'll want to "tighten up," limiting yourself to better hands. Some hands, like small pocket pairs and suited connectors, do better against large fields of opponents, for reasons that will become evident later in this chapter.

Learning the right time and place to play certain hands is one of poker's never-ending challenges.

POSITION, POSITION, POSITION

Here's an experiment to try if you're already playing online poker: Log onto the site and join a very low-limit game—a 5¢/10¢ table will do just fine. Now put a strip of black tape on your monitor, covering your hole cards.

If players seem to be raising too many pots, re-raise from late position. If they are playing in a very straightforward manner—betting if they've connected with the flop, checking if they've missed—call them when you're in late position. Once the flop comes down, you can fold when they bet and bet when they don't. If you pay careful attention to the way the other players are betting and use your position "correctly" (i.e., in a way that maximizes its value), you may be able to beat this game, even without ever seeing your own cards!

"THERE'S NO POINT IN RAISING UNTIL YOU SEE THE FLOP"

Ace-king, or as poker players call it, **Big Slick**, is a very powerful hand. Flop an ace or a king, and you've not only got the top pair, but the best possible kicker to boot. A straight made with Big Slick is a nut straight—someone's going to need a flush or better to beat you. Ace-king, almost every poker book will tell you, is a hand you raise with before the flop.

Over half of the time you play Big Slick, however, the flop is going to miss you completely. You'll often see people at the table who, after playing ace-king "by the book," shake their head in disgust at a jack-high flop, wondering why they bothered raising with it in the first place. Wouldn't it have been smarter just to have **limped** in? Some players will tell you that they *never* raise before the flop with Big Slick—why waste extra money before you've seen a flop?

Once again, there's more to this story. Here are some very good reasons for raising before the flop:

1. **You have a strong hand.** If you knew a particular stock was likely to outperform some of the others in your portfolio, you'd want to invest more of your money in its shares. The same thinking applies to **premium hands**, especially those in Group One—you may not win with them all of the time, but they'll certainly make the best hand more often than almost any other holding. Take advantage of the "investment opportunity" and get more money into the pot.

2. **You want to narrow the field.** Pocket aces will beat almost any other hand, in a one-on-one contest, about 80 percent

of the time. Against two opponents, however, their dominance shrinks to just over 70 percent—there are more ways for someone to connect strongly with the board. Put those aces up against several opponents, and the odds of winning may drop to less than 50 percent. When you raise (or re-raise) before the flop, you'll often scare off some players who would have called a single bet, limiting the number of players involved in a pot, increasing your chances of winning. There is also a possibility of knocking everyone out of the hand before it starts, winning the blinds without a contest. Remember that it's always better to win a small pot than to lose a big one.

3. **You want to isolate a weaker opponent.** If a single player, who you know will limp in (or even raise) with all kinds of less-than-playable hands, has entered the pot, and you estimate that a raise (or a re-raise) has a good chance of knocking out all of the players behind you, it's often a good idea to fire away with any better-than-average hand. If it works, you'll find yourself heads-up against the weak player with advantageous position throughout.

4. **All the players in front of you have folded.** It's usually tough to decide on a course of action from early position, as there are still a lot of players left to act, some of whom could wake up with very strong hands. As the players in front of you fold, however, the odds of your hand being the best hand start to increase. It's often good poker, if you find yourself the first person to act, to raise with hands in late position that you wouldn't consider playing under the gun.

5. **You want your opponents to think you have a strong hand.** The effects of a **pre-flop** raise aren't limited to the opponents you scare off—your early display of strength encourages your opponents to tread lightly after the flop. They might check in situations where they would ordinarily bet, and fold in those where they might call. In a point we'll make throughout the book, poker rewards aggression, and there's no more aggressive statement you can make before the flop than coming in with a raise.

It's almost always a good idea to raise (and, very often, to re-raise) before the flop with a Group One hand. The better your position, the wider the range of hands you can consider raising with. If everyone's folded to you on the button, for example, you can raise with just about anything you think has a better-than-average chance of winning.

However, there are also times where you should be less inclined to throw in a pre-flop raise:

1. **Someone else has already raised.** Unless you've got a great read on an opponent's style of play, it's a good idea to take his or her raises seriously. Many professional players' default response to a pre-flop raise is to look for a reason to fold.

2. **You don't want to narrow the field.** Connectors and suited cards are generally considered **drawing hands**. In other words, you have a much better chance of flopping cards that will get you part of the way to a flush or a straight than you do of flopping a made hand: You're going to have to "draw" cards on the turn, and the possibly the river, in the hopes of getting there. These are more speculative investments, meaning you want to risk less up front while keeping more of your opponents involved, aiming for a bigger-than-normal reward should you make your hand. We'll get into how to evaluate these kinds of situations in the next section.

3. **Your raises aren't working.** Very often—especially early in your poker career, amidst the bloody mayhem of "No Fold'em Hold'em"—you'll find yourself at a table where your raises seem to do the opposite of what you intended. Not only will your opponents refuse to respect the authority of your double-bet, but they'll trip over one another in their hurry to get their money into the growing pot, sometimes raising, re-raising, and **capping** the betting in the hopes of creating an enormous payday. Enormous pots can be problematic: They create incentive for players to hang around until the end with all kinds of otherwise

unlikely propositions. A table full of people drawing on unlikely propositions is likely to result in a gut-wrenching defeat. In these wild games, it *is* often a good idea to wait until you see the flop before investing too much money into the hand.

THE WHEN, THE WHY, AND THE HOW OF POKER

So far, this chapter has been focused on the "When" of poker. When should I play a hand? When should I chase a draw? When should I fold?

Understanding the When of poker is like a toddler learning right from wrong. It's an essential building block of any player's education.

There comes a point, however, when that toddler is going to ask "Why?" A complicated question in the real world, to be sure, but a relatively easy question to answer at the poker table:

To win, on the hands that you win, as much money as possible, and to lose, on the hands that you lose, as little money as possible.

Reread the previous sentence. Let it settle in. This is the Why of poker.

Simple advice, right? You'd be amazed at how many of your opponents will ignore it. (We'll get into some of the other motivations that drive these players in Chapter Six.)

Now that you have a grasp on the When and the Why, you're ready to take on the How.

THE TOOLBOX

Every carpenter uses a hammer and nails. No plumber is without a selection of wrenches. Poker players have their own set of tools. Some are certainly more powerful than others, but there's a time to use each of them. The How of poker is accomplished by knowing which tool will best suit the particular task in front of you.

FOLDING

This is the flathead screwdriver in your box, the tool you'll use most often. At a full table, you'll probably be folding at least two out of every three hands before the flop, and a significant percentage of your hands once you see (and fail to connect with) those first three cards.

Many of your opponents will perceive folding as a sign of weakness, or of your being an all-around tight-ass. They're wrong (about the weakness, anyway)—folding is probably the most powerful tool at your disposal.

Remember the Why of poker. You're looking not just to maximize the amount that you win, but to *minimize what you lose.* Nothing accomplishes that better than folding your hand and waiting for a better spot to play. Find the love of folding, and you'll discover its rewards will be plentiful.

BETTING AND RAISING

At the risk of stretching the metaphor thin, these are your power tools. If your hand is good enough to call a bet, you should strongly consider betting yourself. If you were thinking about betting, and someone's beat you to it, give serious thought to raising.

Betting or raising is almost always superior to just calling. When you call, you have only one way to win: Your hand has to be the best hand. Bet or raise, however, and there are suddenly two ways to come out on top: Your opponent may fold (sometimes, on your better days, with a hand that's got you beat); and even if he doesn't, you may wind up with the best hand.

This is the tool you use when the situation requires aggression, a mind-set that poker has a funny way of rewarding (more on this in Chapter Five).

CHECKING AND CALLING

This is the weakest tool in your kit. There are all kinds of nicknames for players who check and call too much, including **ATM**, **fish**, and **pigeon**. Almost every poker book you read will have something negative to say about calling. "Raise or fold" is a mantra for many winning players.

That being said, it's a tool that does have its uses. Let's say the flop hits you, but weakly—maybe you have top pair with a weak kicker. Or the board looks like it could have made a flush or a straight for someone other than you. If there are several players to act behind you, discretion should be your watchword. Wait and see what everyone else does before committing any money to the pot.

If you are on the come, drawing to a better hand (with the correct pot odds, of course) against opponents who are unlikely to fold to your bet or raise, calling is usually the proper course of action.

It's also occasionally correct to just check and call against superaggressive opponents who like to push their mediocre holdings or flat-out bluff. This is especially true on the river, when, if you think there's any chance of your hand being the best hand, it's almost always worth calling a bet. (Think about it in terms of pot odds: You generally only have to be "right" a small percentage of the time for this to be a profitable play.)

Checking and calling on the river can also be a good way to induce a bluff from your opponent. A good rule of thumb: *If the only way your opponent can call your bet is if he or she has got you beat, then it's usually better to check and call.*

For example, say you hold J♥ 10♦♠ and the board is

J♣ 7♥♥ 6♥ ♥ 4♥ ♥ 3♥ ♥

Your jack-high flush may very well be the best hand, but it's unlikely that your opponent would call a bet with a hand that's worse than yours. If you check, an aggressive player might believe that you don't have a heart and bet into you. You'll win an extra bet if your hand is good, and you've saved yourself from having to call your opponent's likely raise should your hand be second best.

BLUFFING

To the uninitiated, poker is all about bluffing. Consider this your initiation—they are wrong! While bluffing is certainly an important part of the game, it's not as effective a play as you may have been led to believe.

In order for a bluff to work, you have to be using it against an opponent who is scared enough or, more importantly, *smart* enough to fold. This is the "Paradox of the Bluff": It's a terrible play to make against terrible opponents.

Limit poker—especially the lower limits—is a show-down game, meaning you very often have to show the best hand to win a pot. Lots of players see flops, and many of them won't be savvy enough to recognize when you have them dominated, let alone when you are *pretending* to have them dominated. *Bluffing in a typical low-limit poker game is generally a complete waste of time—and money.*

When you do bluff, you'd prefer to be doing it against as few opponents as possible—one is best—minimizing the chances that someone has a hand that they *just have to call you* with. It's pretty pointless to bluff against maniacs or morons, so limit the play to your opponents who show weakness, or at least some sign of paying attention to the way you conduct yourself at the table.

One good time to bluff is when a **scare card** appears on the board. For example, say you call a raise from the blind with 10♥ 9♥, and the flop comes

J♥ 6♠ 2♦

You check to Raising Ray, who also checks. You've been watching Ray long enough to guess that he's probably got a hand like ace-king or ace-queen, but is afraid that you might have connected with the board. Now the turn card is the J♠. This is a very scary card for Ray—he has no way of knowing that he's got the best hand—and represents a great situation to bluff at the pot.

Your bluffs don't have to work every time to have a positive expectation—one success can more than make up for three or four failures. It's also not a bad idea to get caught bluffing every once in a while, as your opponents will be more likely to give you action the next time you actually hold a legitimate hand.

SEMI-BLUFFING

A **semi-bluff** is a bet or a raise made with a hand that, while not currently the best, has a chance of getting there. If your opponents fold, fantastic; if they don't, you still have a decent shot of drawing to a winning hand.

Semi-bluffing is most often used to get a "free card" on a more expensive street. For example, let's say you're dealt A♣ K♣ on the button. A player in early position limps in. You raise. The Big Blind and the early position player—let's call her Limping Lucy—both call. Now the flop comes . . .

J♣ 7♦ 3♣

. . . and Lucy bets into you. This is a great time for a semi-bluff raise. While she may very well have a better hand than you at the moment, you have nine outs to a nut flush, plus another six outs to an ace or a king that might also make you the best hand. Your raise will probably encourage the Big Blind, confronted with a double-sized bet, to fold, and you may scare Lucy off as well. Even if she calls, she'll likely check to you on the turn. If the turn card makes your hand, you can go ahead and bet it. If it doesn't, you can check behind her, getting a "free" look at the river card.

In other words, by investing an extra small bet on the flop, you've saved yourself from having to call a big bet on the turn. Note that for this play to be effective, you have to be in later position than the original bettor—one more example of how important having good position is to a skilled poker player.

Also keep in mind that many veteran players are hip to the old semi-bluff for a free card, and may re-raise you and bet into you on the turn, nullifying the "discount" you were looking for.

CHECK-RAISING

As the name suggests, the move involves checking in front of an opponent or opponents in the hope that one (or more) of them makes a bet. When the action gets back to you, you raise. It's generally a good idea to be holding a very strong hand when you do, as many players like to call down check-raisers "just to see," and the increased money in the pot can sometimes create situations where it becomes correct for your opponents to call with all kinds of crazy draws.

The play has endured some criticism over the years— some players of old believed that this particular type of duplicity constituted bad manners—but in today's game, the check-raise is an undeniably valuable tool, helping you to extract the most money possible with your winning hands. It also may be one of the most overused.

You have to be very confident that someone is going to bet behind you. If no one takes the bait, not only have you failed to make any money from this particular street, but you've given all of your opponents a dreaded free card, possibly allowing them to draw out on you. When in doubt, it's almost always better just to bet your stronger hands.

Check-raising is most effective against one other opponent, especially when a seemingly innocuous card has helped you, or when you want to "clear the field" with a double-bet.

For example, let's say you call from early position with

[10♣] [10♥]. Limping Lucy, seated in middle position, calls behind you, before Raising Ray ups it to two bets from the button. The blinds fold; Lucy calls. Now the flop comes . . .

[K♠] [10♦] [9♣]

Your set of tens is probably in the lead right now. Rather than betting out, however, the wiser play is to check to Raising Ray, who seems likely to bet, then raise when the action gets back to you. Not only will you get more money into the pot, but by confronting Lucy with a double-sized bet, you may get her to throw away a potentially dangerous hand that otherwise might have been worth a call, like [K♦] [J♦] or [Q♠] [10♠].

SLOWPLAYING

Sometimes a flop hits you so hard and looks so menacing that any aggression on your part will scare off your opponents. By **slowplaying**, or passively checking and calling on the early streets, you can sometimes lure opponents into making ill-advised bets and raises on the later, more expensive streets.

This is the tool most abused by new poker players, who fall in love with the idea of being able to trap their opponents.* For one thing, it's always dangerous to give free cards—very few hands are such absolute locks that your opponents will be **drawing dead.** Secondly, your opponents are often more

---

* **Fancy Play Syndrome**, or FPS, is a condition that afflicts many new (and quite a few experienced) players. Its primary symptoms are the overuse of the more specialized tools like check-raising and slowplaying, missing opportunities to extract extra bets while giving potentially dangerous free cards to their opponents. Straightforward poker—betting when you have the best hand, folding when you don't—may seem boring, but it's generally the most profitable way to play the game.

likely to call a bet on the flop than on the more expensive turn or river, meaning that you may be sacrificing your only opportunity to milk any money out of them.

The best time to slowplay is when your hand is not only a cinch or near-cinch to win, but when allowing your opponents to take a free card offers a decent chance of making them a *second-best hand.*

For example, say you're dealt [4♣ ♣] [4♦ ♦] in late position. Limping Lucy calls in front of you. You raise. Both the blinds call. So does Lucy. The flop comes

[10♥ ♥] [4♠ ♠] [4♥ ♥]

You have four of a kind, virtually unbeatable. Everyone checks to you. A bet here will likely win the pot. Check, however, and all kinds of good things might happen to you on fourth street. Maybe Lucy, who was afraid to bet into the flop with her [10♣ ♣] [9♦ ♦], finds the courage to take a stab. An ace or king may give someone a big pair. On your best days, the turn card winds up making a flush for one opponent and a full house for another, setting up a raising war from which you will come away victorious — and substantially wealthier.

Before moving on, take note of how specific these conditions were. If the flop had instead come . . .

[10♥ ♥] [9♠ ♠] [4♥ ♥]

. . . granting a free card to your opponents would be a terrible mistake, as trip fours are dog meat should someone make a straight or a flush.

WINNING LOW-LIMIT HOLD'EM

by Lee Jones

Who is Lee Jones? A great tournament champion? A fearless competitor in ultra-high-stakes cash games? A genius in the mathematics of poker?

The answer is (d), none of the above. He's a computer programmer from San Jose, California, who happened to write an incredibly useful book for poker newbies.

While there's no denying the genius of Sklansky and Malmuth, their works presuppose that your level of competition has some sense of how to play the game.* Unfortunately, your early sorties at the poker table will likely pit you against people who, to put it nicely, don't have a clue. They will play too many hands. They won't know when to fold. They will make all kinds of "mistakes" that can actually wind up costing *you* a lot of money if you aren't prepared for them.

Jones puts a lot of emphasis on "reading the board." To succeed at low-limit poker, you've got to examine a flop with the idea that one or more opponents have already made some kind of hand, or at least picked up a draw. His book helps you learn how to value your hand in relation to the cards that are out there, enabling you

---

* In response to the growing popularity of the low-limit game, Sklansky and Malmuth recently teamed with one Ed Miller to release a book called *Small Stakes Hold 'em: Winning Big with Expert Play*.

to make better decisions about when and how to proceed.

While *Winning Low-Limit Hold'em* shouldn't be the last book you read on poker, you could do a lot worse than making it one of the first.

OTHER FORMS OF PRACTICE

If you're looking to hone your skills before testing them out on a live opponent, you might find it helpful to get some practice against a simulator.

There are all kinds of computer simulations out there, from virtual casinos to small applets you can play on your Palm Pilot. Unfortunately, most computers generally don't play a very good game of Texas Hold'em (see page 61).

The best of the bunch seem to be the "Turbo" series of programs developed by Bob Wilson, poker player, software entrepreneur, and longtime member of Mensa. The artificial intelligence governing the play is pretty good, and a fairly sophisticated set of controls allow you to customize the individual playing style of each virtual opponent you'll face. The Wilson programs are expensive—they currently retail for about $90 a pop—but his Web site (*www.wilsonsoftware.com*) is full of testimonials from real people promising that you'll quickly recoup the investment through your improved play.

THE COMPUTER HAND

It's another one of those stories that reeks of being anecdotal, but it has managed to linger around long enough to earn its own place in poker lore. Apparently someone, somewhere, at some time, ran a computer simulation to see which hands in Texas Hold'em were worth playing. As the legend goes, this computer revealed that Q-7 was the worst of the profitable hands.

In actuality, Q-7—which still carries the nickname of "the computer hand"—is a pretty awful holding, and there's not a winning poker player in the world who would play it with any regularity. The story does, however, illuminate the difficulties of using computers to figure things out about poker, a game that's perhaps a little too nuanced for our current crop of machines.

HOW TO THINK LIKE A POKER PLAYER

Poker players are a wily breed. Like there's any choice. While the fluctuations of Lady Luck can make Vanderbilts out of madmen and turn sane, responsible players into broken, wrecked vestiges of humanity, the truth is that over the long haul, only the strong survive.

Which raises the question, what makes a strong poker player? Is it cleverness, or daring? A razor-sharp mathematical mind, or a deep understanding of human psychology?

It's safe to say that all of these qualities in some way or another contribute to the makeup of a top-notch player. But perhaps more important than any of these individual traits is something that we'll call the poker mind-set. That is, how to think like a poker player.

WHY DO WE PLAY?

> *In my younger and more vulnerable years my father gave me some advice that I've been turning over in my mind ever since. "Whenever you feel like criticizing anyone," he told me, "just remember that all the people in the world haven't had the advantages that you've had."*
>
> — F. SCOTT FITZGERALD, *The Great Gatsby*

You're sitting in a low-limit hold'em game. It's late, you're **stuck,** and you haven't seen a playable hand in what seems like hours. Meanwhile, the guy across the table from you—let's call him "the Drunk"—is playing every hand he's dealt and is winning way more than his fair share of them, knocking down another beer with each large pot that he rakes in.

A new deal. Several players limp in before you, on the button, look down to find a suited ace-king. You raise, the blinds fold, the limpers all call, building a nice little pot.

The flop comes A-9-4 **rainbow.** So far, so good. Everyone checks to you. You bet, leading all of your opponents to fold. That is, except for the Drunk, who obviously hasn't paid a lick of attention to the tight **table image** (more on what this is below) you've been maintaining all night. "What the heck!" he says as he calls.

The turn card brings a beautiful king, giving you top two pair. The Drunk checks to you, and you bet. He takes a swig of his beer, tosses in enough chips to call, and gazes to the heavens. "Gimme a deuce!" he yells.

The dealer lays down the river card. Sure enough, it's a deuce. The Drunk slaps the table, lets out a laugh of unrestrained joy, and throws in a bet. Every instinct tells you that, somehow, he has you beat, but you make the crying call.

He flips over pocket deuces—giving him a set over your two pair—and starts piling the chips, *your chips*. Your vision starts to get hazy. How could he have called you? He only had two outs!

Experienced players will recognize this tale as a classic bad beat story. You were a 22-to-1 favorite (96 percent) going into the river! How, you might ask yourself, could the Drunk have been such an idiot as to call?

Setting aside for a moment any issue of the Drunk's intelligence, a better question to ask might be, "What are the psychological factors that contributed to the Drunk's decision to chase such an improbable **suckout**?"

Everyone has a different set of reasons for playing poker. Some players enjoy the social interaction. Others enjoy the contest of wills, the chance to prove that he or she is smarter, braver, or sneakier than everyone else at the table. A good many of the players you'll face (especially at the lower limits) love to gamble, thriving on the feeling that fate, luck, destiny, and/or the spiritual being of choice is shining some divine light on them, if only for a fleeting moment.

A winning poker player recognizes—and takes advantage of—the motivations that drive others to play the game. The *social butterflies* like to be liked, are often reluctant to bluff, and are prone to showing you when they've got the goods (thus saving you a bet on the end). The *ego-*

tists can be led into making mistakes, overplaying some hands while costing themselves bets in an effort to make fancy plays that prove how clever they are. As for the *gamblers,* well, luck eventually runs out . . . hopefully, before they've taken all of your money.

These types of players face a huge disadvantage when they encounter a poker player who is motivated by one unwavering goal: *to win money.* This isn't to say that you shouldn't be social, make fancy plays, or take some chances, as long as you're doing it to win more money.

Good poker players rarely criticize their opponent's play—you don't want to scare suckers from the table, or even worse, motivate them to start playing better. Think of it this way: When you're at a pet store, there is almost always a sign that says: DON'T TAP ON THE AQUARIUM.

The best players know how to "train" their adversaries. Raising before the flop with a junk hand (which you later show down, hopefully as you're raking in the chips) is a good way to get your opponents to pay you off those times you're holding a legitimate hand. Another example is to "always" play a hand a certain way—for example, consistently raising with a draw to a flush—then suddenly doing the opposite. The goal is not only to keep your opponents off-balance, but to keep them off-balance in a predictable way.

Of course, your more skilled opponents will not only know that you are trying to train them, but will be trying their hardest to do the same to you.

WHAT KIND OF PLAYER ARE YOU?

Poker games—and the people who play them—can generally be described with two sets of competing adjectives: loose or tight, passive or aggressive.

A **loose** player plays a lot of different starting hands, often disregarding strategic considerations like position or the raise in front of them. A **tight** player, in contrast, plays very few hands, waiting patiently for what seem to be the most opportune moments to enter a pot. By extension, a loose game features a lot of players in every pot, while in a tight game, each hand is generally contested by only two or three players.

A **passive** player tends to check and call, usually content to let others take the lead unless he or she has the absolute nuts. **Aggressive** players are proponents of the "raise or fold" philosophy of poker, the virtues of which are expounded upon later in this chapter. A passive game offers a lot of checking and calling, while an aggressive game boasts more raising and re-raising.

Most newcomers start out as loose and passive. Poker veterans will sometimes refer to this type of player as a **calling station** or an ATM (as in "**cash machine**").

You'll encounter many players who like to play

loose and aggressive. They are the gamblers, bluffing frequently and occasionally winning with all kinds of **junk** hands. They also tend to go broke. (On your bad days, however, these types of players demonstrate a most unpleasant tendency to break *you* in the process.)

Tight-passive players are often called **rocks,** as it's about as easy to win money from them, so the expression goes, as it is to draw blood from a stone. The good news is that you really have to bend over backward to lose money to this type of player: When a rock bets, he or she can be counted on to have the goods.

Most poker players strive to be tight and aggressive. They choose their battles carefully, looking for those situations where they have the best of it. Once engaged in battle, they are tenacious fighters, raising and re-raising with ferocious (but controlled) aggression.

There are exceptions to this rule. Gus Hansen, for one, is a player who has had a lot of success with a loose-aggressive style. It's a difficult style to play well, but can be even more difficult to defend against. This may sound counterintuitive, but as your level of skill increases, you can actually begin to play more hands before the flop, as your decision-making will be superior to your opponents. You'll extract extra bets on the hands you win, and escape cheaply those times you run into trouble.

Don't fall into the common trap of overestimating

your poker skills—you're not Gus Hansen yet. Playing tight-aggressive poker is a winning strategy and the one you should employ.

EVERYTHING IS ZEN

It's just a job. Grass grows, birds fly, waves pound the sand. I just beat people up.

—MUHAMMAD ALI

There's a poker adage that goes something like, "If you can't play with a smile, then don't play at all."

Whoever originally said this obviously was miraculously enlightened, utterly insane, or benefiting from some very effective medication. No one can play happy all of the time. There will be hands, sessions, weeks—even months—when the luck of the cards seems to be running against you. When every maniac seemingly intent on losing his or her bankroll to your solid, steady play manages to hit that miracle card (or, when things are really bad, two running cards) to crack your pocket aces.

The great poker players know that bad beats are an inevitable part of the game. Examined from a slightly different angle, *most* of your beats should be bad beats, as you're generally pouring money into the pot in those situations when you already have the best of it, or at least have the right pot odds to hang around for a draw. What's more, you should *want* your opponents to play badly. Yes, it sucks when someone hits a 22-to-1 long shot against you. Over the long haul, however, you should be pocketing his or her desperate money the other 21 times.

Experienced poker players know this, and most have learned to combat any feelings of despair with a Zen-like consciousness. Hands come, hands go. You just play poker.

Not unlike the mastery of Zen, this kind of inner peace comes only with practice. When asked what it feels like to lose $100,000 in a single session, Jennifer Harman offered this reply:

> "You don't even think about it. But, you know, it's hard getting to this frame of mind, believe me. . . . The first time I lost $3,000, I went home and cried like a baby. . . . When I lost $10,000, same thing. When I lost $30,000, I couldn't sleep for four days. When I lost $100,000, for the first time in my life, I couldn't sleep for a week. But then, the next time I lost $100,000, and the next time I lost $100,000, you know, it's like your pain threshold just goes up."

This "letting go" isn't just applied to losing sessions, but to individual hands as well. One of the hardest concepts for a new player to grasp is the idea that once you've thrown your chips into the center of the table, your connection to them has ended. Regardless of how much a professional player has personally "invested" in any particular pot, he or she will continue to make or call bets only as long as the odds of winning the pot justify further investment. Laying down a once-powerful hand in the face of overwhelming evidence that it's become second-best is a sign of a good poker player.

Keep the acronym H.A.L.T. near the top of your mind. If you are Hungry, Angry, Lonely, or Tired, you shouldn't be at the table. As poker author John Fox once wrote, "The best player in the world with a temporarily dulled brain is not even a match for an average player using full concentration." Save yourself the embarrassment of blowing your bankroll in a less-than-tip-top state of mind—simply HALT.

ZEN AND THE ART OF POKER
by Larry W. Phillips

This journey to poker enlightenment starts with a quote from *Caddyshack*, "Be the ball," perhaps fooling you into believing that the information you are holding in your hands is at best humorous, at worst trivial. It's both, of course, which is what makes this little book so powerful.

Phillips, a writer, journalist, and longtime poker player, uses quotes from Sun Tzu to Chuck Norris to illuminate one hundred truths about the game, from "Learn to use inaction as a weapon" to "Make sure you know when you're on a cold streak." An entertaining read, to be sure, but also a deceptively insightful lesson in developing a poker mind-set.

GAME SELECTION

*I don't care to belong to any club that will have me as a
member.*

—GROUCHO MARX

Imagine being the ninth best poker player in the world. It
would feel pretty good, right? Sure it would, unless you're
sitting at a table with the eight players who are better than
you. Perhaps the most important decision a poker player
has to make is whether or not to sit down at a particular
game.

First, you need to consider your opposition. As the
cliché goes, if you can't spot the fish, it's probably you.
Make sure that there is at least one person who is stupid,
exhausted, desperate, irrational, and/or drunk enough for
you to outplay.

You also have to compare the tone of the game with
your personal style of play. If you are someone who just
loves to bluff, you're not going to do very well in a game of
loose, passive players who will call you all the way to a
showdown. If you are a patient, calculating sort, you're
going to do best against those Type As who will raise your
nut hands on the final street.

Remember that you'll likely make a lot more money in a
lower stakes game that you can run over than you will in a
higher stakes game where you have to fight for every chip.

Almost as important as selecting the right game is
choosing the best seat. A game that is eminently beatable
from one side of the table may be tragically unprofitable if
you find yourself in the wrong chair. This isn't about

superstition—despite what you'll often hear from your fellow players, there's no such thing as a "cold" seat—but about position, which you've already discovered to be one of the most important aspects of the game.

You generally want the hyperaggressive players on your right and the tight-ass rocks on your left. When the maniac comes into the pot, you will re-raise and "isolate" him from the tight-ass rocks, who will likely fold to your double-sized bet. You'll play for pots heads-up, in superior position, and—assuming you're not a maniac yourself when it comes to hand selection—usually with a hand that's a favorite to win.

Now look at what would happen were the situation reversed, with the tight rocks on your right and the maniac on your left. Every time you enter the pot, the maniac raises or re-raises, while the rocks—who are no strangers to the isolation strategy—won't be afraid to re-raise. Now it's *you* who will be facing a double raise, often out of position. Change your seat, even if it means getting up from the game!

Any time there are multiple open seats at a table when you arrive, take a few minutes to figure out which will be the most profitable. Your win rate depends on it.

BANKROLL

When I have to put my money out there, my money's out there. Everybody knows that. . . . So if you want to mess with me, it's going to cost you. . . . You have to be willing to die in order to live in these tournaments. . . . That's basically it.
—AMIR VAHEDI, *ESPN's 2003 World Series of Poker*

This philosophy, which has served Vahedi so well—he's one of the world's best no-limit hold'em players—applies to any and all levels of play. A poker player should be always be concentrating on winning, and never *not losing*. "Scared money" rarely wins, especially against aggressive players who are able to recognize it. Poker is a game of critical decisions. It's not easy to make these decisions when their outcome could affect your ability to pay the rent or put dinner on the table.

As Chip Reese once said of a fellow Poker Hall of Famer: "If you think about what money can do for you, you're gone. That's what made Stuey Ungar such a great no-limit player: He never, ever, *ever* cared."*

A good rule of thumb is this: If you can't say to yourself "they're only chips" as you fling a bet into the pot, then you are probably playing in a game beyond your means.

As we've mentioned previously, conventional wisdom suggests that you should be willing to lose (and thus ready to play) twenty times more than the maximum bet. However, there's more to choosing a limit than just bankroll. Limit games are generally divided into three basic categories, each with its own psychology (or, some might say, psychosis).

LOW-LIMIT GAMES

Low-limit games, ranging from 10¢/20¢ to $6/12, are generally populated by players who are new to the game, aren't good enough to compete for higher stakes, or are playing for the sheer fun of it. As a result, you tend to see

---

* Yes, there is a Poker Hall of Fame at Binion's Horseshoe, which has been inducting a new player each year since its inception in 1979.

people playing too many hands and taking them too far. Winning at the lower limits requires a great deal of patience and a strong understanding of pot odds—you're going to make most of your money by making "good" decisions (i.e., mathematically correct) while forcing your opponents to make "bad" ones. It generally doesn't make sense to do a lot of bluffing in these games, because for a bluff to be successful, you've got to be playing against people who are willing to fold. Nor is it particularly useful to make a lot of fancy plays, as your opponents are unlikely to respond to (or even notice) your artistry. Because most of the players are going to be involved in most of the pots, chasing miraculous cards, the odds are much better that one or two of them will actually make their hands, meaning that you are going to take a lot of bad beats.

Most experienced players view low-limit poker as something akin to working in a salt mine. It's hard work, occasionally painful, and—once the basic concepts are grasped—pretty damn boring. But for new players, there's no substitute for this kind of initiation. Keep in mind that a good poker player will, more times than not, utterly destroy low-limit games. If you can't win consistently at these games, don't be so quick to blame the bad beats— you probably have some more work to do before you move up.

MIDDLE-LIMIT GAMES

This term is used to describe that narrow but popular range of games between $10/20 and $80/160. Generally, you'll be facing other players who are pretty good and/or have a lot of money to lose. You'll need all of the skills that helped you to win at the lower limits—a **leak** in your game that cost you a few dollars a session in the smaller games will cost you hundreds, if not thousands, in a middle-limit contest. What really distinguishes this game, however, is the emphasis on bankroll and the ability to wield it aggressively. From a psychological standpoint, it's quite a different experience to toss in a $60 bet than one for $6, and losing $3,000 feels a lot worse than losing $300. Your opponents know this, and will repeatedly "put you to the test," raising and re-raising with marginal hands or draws to see if you have the guts to call or, more importantly, throw in your own raises and re-raises. You need to approach a middle-limit game with a bankroll that can withstand these attacks and allow you to play with fearlessness.

HIGH-LIMIT GAMES

These are the games where legends are made while small fortunes are routinely exchanged. The term "high-limit" is used to describe games from $100/200 on up, but as you might guess, the difference in average pot size between a $200/400 and a $50,000/100,000 game (yes, one was recently run at the Bellagio in Las Vegas) is, in an understatement, substantial. In fact, this category is occasionally further delineated to include an "ultra-high-limit" game, but the basic principles of either are the same.

You'll of course need the same skills and fearlessness that allowed you to succeed at the lower and medium level games, but you'll have to supplement your play with a superior understanding of human psychology.

High-limit poker is a game of psychological levels. At the most basic level, there's the hand you have, and the hand you think your opponent has. Ratchet this up a notch, and start to consider the hand your opponent thinks that you have, and the hand that your opponent thinks that you think he or she has. It's possible to take this kind of thinking to even higher levels. In short, certain plays that would seem absolutely idiotic at one level of thinking might be considered sublime masterpieces of deception when examined through the filter of a higher level.

The trick, of course, is determining which level of thinking your opponent is using (and, in turn, the level your opponent *wants* you to believe that he or she is using.) As you might guess, the result can often be a labyrinthine battle of wits to make your head explode. Many top players are thus adherents of **game theory,** the branch of mathematics devoted to the study of really, really complex decision-making. In its most sophisticated practice, game theorists will make certain decisions *totally at random* in order to confuse their opponents.

Take a minute to let that sink in: You're wagering thousands, even millions, of dollars on the basis of completely random decisions. This is high-limit poker.

THE VIRTUE OF AGGRESSION

Check, check, check, chicken!
—A COMMON POKER TAUNT

If there is one "X-factor" that unites all great poker players, it's their willingness to play aggressive poker.

Like it or not, aggression seems to have a magical effect at most poker tables. A strong raise is usually better than a mere call, and when you can't raise, folding should at least be seriously considered.

There are many reasons why aggression is such a force to be reckoned with. Here are a few:

Aggression forces your opponents to react.

Nobody likes to make tough decisions. When you are able to take control of the betting, you make the other guy guess, worry, and, when things are going your way, lay down a better hand than yours.

Aggression lets you know where you stand.

While it's not always the most cost-efficient way of acquiring information from your opponents, it is usually the most effective. A player who calls your raise is often on a draw, or has a made hand that he or she is not so confident about. An opponent's re-raise or check-raise should be acknowledged as a sign of strength, usually denoting a powerful made hand or an excellent draw.

Aggression gets you "free cards" and prevents you from giving them away.

As discussed in the previous chapter, a well-timed bet or raise before the flop or on an early street can let you see a card on a later, more expensive street, for free, occasionally allowing you to improve your hand. The opposite is also true—it's generally an error of the worst kind to allow your opponent to see a free card when you have the best hand.

Aggression can turn a second-best hand into a drawing hand.

Here's an example: In a $6/12 Texas Hold'em game, an early position player comes in for a raise. A player in middle position calls the $12 bet. Everyone else folds to you in the small blind, where you discover pocket queens and decide to re-raise to $18. The big blind calls, as do the other two players, creating a $72 pot.

The flop comes A-K-10, far from ideal for your queens. You bet, the big blind calls, the original raiser *raises,* causing the player in middle position to fold.

You're pretty sure at this point that you have the second best hand, as the raiser's bound to have an ace or a king, possibly even three of a kind. But should you fold? Thanks to your aggressive betting, not only do you have a pretty good idea of where you stand, but the $96 in the pot makes it correct for you to do something that your grandfather warned you never to do: draw for the inside straight. Sure, the odds against you hitting a jack on the turn are about 12-to-1, but you're getting 16-to-1 from the pot. Aggression has "magically" transformed your hand into a worthwhile draw.

THE INNER VOICE

I felt a great disturbance in the Force.
— SIR ALEC GUINNESS AS BEN "OBI-WAN" KENOBI,
Star Wars

All of the great poker players have it: an inner voice. It tells them when their opponent is weak, and it can be moved off a hand with a well-timed bluff. Or it acts as an alarm bell, signaling darker menace in what, on the surface, seemed to be an innocuous call.

Some call it ESP. Others attribute it to some preternatural awareness of fear, hormones, or vibrational energy. Rationalists will claim that the ability to "sense" that something is wrong is just the ability, acquired with years of experience, to recognize a subtle inconsistency in the way things should normally play out.

Whatever it is, you need to learn it. Once you've learned to hear this inner voice, you're ready to embark on the even greater challenge of listening to it.

THERE'S NO "ALWAYS" IN POKER

A foolish consistency is the hobgoblin of little minds.
— RALPH WALDO EMERSON

Contrary to what some books (and even more players) will tell you, the only "right" way to play poker is the way that consistently wins you money.

Even if that means being inconsistent.

♥ ♦ ♣ ♠ ♥ ♦ ♣ ♠ ♥ ♦ ♣ ♠ ♥ ♦ ♣ ♠ ♥ ♦ ♣ ♠ ♥ ♦ ♣ ♠

YOUR DEFINING MOMENT

You've arrived about two hours late to a $10/20 home game hosted by your golf pro. Five players are seated at a small table, and to your surprise there are no empty chairs.

"Glad you could make it!" says the Pro. "Five-hundred-dollar buy-in, if you can handle it. My kid will grab an extra chair from upstairs . . . we'll make room for you."

You have about five minutes to decide where you want the chair to go. Being the aspiring professional that you are, you study the table, the action, and the players in between bites of cracker with cheese dip.

Seat 1: The Pro. $500 in chips. He's drinking Budweiser.

Seat 2: The Cartboy. $200. Coke.

Seat 3: The Greenskeeper. $650. Clear liquid.

Seat 4: The Caddy: $800. Clear liquid w/a slice of lime.

Seat 5: The Bartender. $350. Something in a martini glass.

The Pro is on the button, the small and big blinds are posted by the Cartboy and the Greenskeeper respectively. You stand behind the Greenskeeper, who lets you peek at his cards—an ace-ten offsuit. The Caddy takes a swig of his drink—"Raise it up, boys, I'm in a rush!" and tosses $20 into the pot. The Bartender and the Pro both call. The Cartboy folds, accidentally exposing his $\boxed{K\clubsuit}$ $\boxed{10\spadesuit}$. The Greenskeeper thinks for a bit but finally folds his hand.

Three-way action.

The flop comes $\boxed{A\clubsuit}$ $\boxed{9\blacklozenge}$ $\boxed{3\blacklozenge}$. The Caddy tosses in a $10 bet. The Bartender shakes his head and calls. The Pro calls quickly, which you know from past experience usually indicates he's on a draw.

The turn is the $\boxed{10\spadesuit}$. The Caddy checks, the Bartender checks, and the Pro stews for a bit and finally checks.

The river brings the $\boxed{J\spadesuit}$. The Caddy quickly fires a bet. "Twenty dollars, boys, twenty dollars." The Bartender calls, as does the pro. It's a showdown.

The board: A♠ 9♦ ♦ 3♦ ♦ 10♦ ♦ J♦

The Caddy shows J♦ 7♦ ♦ for a flush.

The Bartender shows J♦ 9♠ ♠ for a slightly better flush.

The Pro opens his A♠ Q♦ , a queen-high flush and the best hand. "Damn," he exclaims as he rakes in the chips. I was afraid that one of you had the king of diamonds."

Pro Jr. arrives with your chair. "Make some room for the new blood!" Where do you ask him to put it?

♥ ♦ ♣ ♠ ♥ ♦ ♣ ♠ ♥ ♦ ♣ ♠ ♥ ♦ ♣ ♠ ♥ ♦ ♣ ♠ ♥ ♦ ♣ ♠

THE ANSWER

You don't have a lot of information about these players, but you have enough to make an educated guess. You recall the mantra, "Maniacs on your right, tight asses on your left."

Clearly the Caddy—who just raised under the gun with jack-seven offsuit—and the Bartender—who called his raise with an unsuited 10-9—are the maniacs of the bunch. The Pro is not only playing squeaky tight, but weak as well, failing to bet or raise with what turned out to be the strongest hand throughout. The Greenskeeper and the Cartboy both threw away playable hands in the face of a raise, signaling tight, tight, tight.

You slide up your chair between the Bartender and the Pro and pop open a beer (just to seem social). You look down at your first hand and find two aces—"pocket rockets." It's looking like your mom will be getting a very, very nice present for Mother's Day.

THE CARDROOM

Man, has poker changed.

Ask a player from an earlier generation to describe the poker scene, and you'll probably hear stories about Texas roadhouses, the backroom of a candy store or after-hours games in the caddyshack at a local golf club. If you were lucky enough to live in a state like California, where poker has long been treated as a legal game of skill, and didn't mind inhaling several metric tons of secondhand smoke, you could test your mettle against a few cold-blooded retirees and shady characters with dubious nicknames like "Artichoke Joe." Otherwise, you were going to have to wait for that trip to Reno or Las Vegas (or Monte

Carlo or Macao) to enter a "professional" gaming establishment.

Today, if you live in the United States, you are likely within driving distance of a full-service cardroom. Some offer gourmet meals, prepared by celebrity chefs. Many are smoke-free. You'll still find your share of shady characters, but they'll be playing alongside successful (and unsuccessful) businesspeople, college students and housewives, even famous actors and actresses.

There are some very good reasons to play in a cardroom. Depending on your area, you're likely to find a variety of games and limits to suit your mood and bankroll. Most of them have state-of-the-art security cameras and professional dealers, making cheating nearly impossible. Perhaps best of all is the chance to escape your circle of regulars and wage psychological warfare (or simply partake in some old-fashioned social interaction) with a diverse cast of characters.

The visit to a cardroom is a must for any serious poker player. Before you jump in the car, however, you might want to consider a few of the disadvantages of casino play. Smaller rooms may not be able to offer a wide selection of games. You're likely to face more serious players representing a tougher challenge than your usual Friday night lineup. And then there are those pesky extra costs—tipping and the rake—that can add up over the course of a session (more on that later).

WHAT TO WEAR

Poker used to be a game that had its own sense of fashion. The original riverboat gamblers were men of style. Perhaps the prototype was Jimmy Fitzgerald, an Irish poker player who, according to Old West historian Robert K. DeArment, traveled up and down the Mississippi porting a wardrobe containing two dozen expensive suits (actually, his three slaves were doing most of the porting), the latest custom-made boots from Paris, and a cascading watch chain some sixteen feet long made of gold spun as thick as his pinkie finger.

The tradition carried on through the 1970s, upheld by such luminaries as Texan Crandall Addington, whose fine play (he placed second in the World Series of Poker in 1978) never interfered with his finer threads—he was known to change his linen suits, silk shirts, designer ties (never loosened), and mink Stetson hats as often as three times a day. Even among the less sartorially splendid players there were certain—let's call them stylistic choices—that could be counted on. Cowboy hats, plaid sports jackets made from potentially hazardous materials, huge pinkie rings, and half-chewed cigars were all *de rigueur.*

While it's hard to believe, fashion in poker has gotten *worse.* The uniform of today's typical Vegas pro seems to consist of ratty sweats, sunglasses, and a baseball cap. The number of slobs you'll see in a poker tournament defies any rational explanation. Paul Magriel, for example, better known to fans of the World Poker Tour as "X-22," has been a National Science Fellow, a chess and backgammon champion, and an Ivy League professor.* When it comes to his wardrobe, however, let's just say that the promotional T-shirts given out at many tournaments actually allow Paul to improve his appearance.

What you do wear goes a long way toward defining your table image. While there's no reason why you can't approach the game with your own sense of style, certain choices do have their virtues.

SUNGLASSES

They say that the eyes are the windows to the soul. The best poker players know this and will stare you down, looking for you to betray your hand with the slightest twitch or blink. Many players will protect themselves from this kind of scrutiny with sunglasses. Some go for sporty (Chris Ferguson's black Oakleys), others opt for elegant (Johnny Chan's black-and-gold Versaces), and some choose straight-up psychedelic (Scottie Ngyuen's purple-tinted shades).

One important thing to keep in mind: Wearing sunglasses at the final table of the World Series can give you the look and edge of a champion. Those same sunglasses at a $2/4 table will probably make you look like a jackass. If you're ever fortunate enough to make the final table of a World Poker Tour event, you'll find that the producers are quite aware of the "jackass" factor and have outlawed sunglasses. Everyone watching on the Travel Channel will get to see the look of fear in your eyes (a false tell, of course) when Phil Hellmuth Jr. stares into your soul, contemplating a raise.

---

* The nickname "X-22" apparently comes from a 64-player chess tournament Magriel waged against himself. X-22 won.

HATS

Just as with sunglasses, a good hat can help hide your face during those gut-wrenching showdowns. The ubiquitous baseball cap is effective, but has almost become cliché. Cowboy hats work best if you're actually from someplace where cowboys still roam. Fishing caps are popular and have a lot of metaphorical significance in a game where "fish" and "fishing" play significant roles. Perhaps the most famous lid of all time was the Lincolnesque stovepipe that Ken "Top Hat" Smith, a utilities contractor and chess master from Dallas, wore to the 1978 World Series. After each winning hand, Smith would tip his cap to the crowd—occasionally while standing on the table—and declare "What a player!" (He finished sixth.)

COMFORTABLE CLOTHES

Poker is a game of sitting relatively motionless for long periods of time . . . interrupted by adrenaline-filled moments of absolute terror. As a result, you'll see very few poker players wearing knotted ties, turtlenecks, crotch-hugging jeans, or any other potential source of discomfort. (Actually, when you do come across a player who's relaxed enough to wear a tie without loosening it, you're looking at someone who isn't too worried about losing money, likely a maniac, a top-notch player, or both. Be afraid, be very afraid.)

Some players favor hooded sweatshirts, hoping to further conceal their features from scrutiny. One guy who may have taken this look too far is Phil Laak, whose hood-and-dark glasses approach has earned him the nickname "Unabomber."

Most pros, however, dress for comfort. Phil Ivey has a seemingly infinite collection of sports jerseys. Paul Darden decks himself out in Phat Farm sweats. Dewey Tomko always looks prepared to make a quick transition to the nearest golf course.

Other players have taken the notion of comfort to ridiculous extremes. Some players play barefoot. It's unlikely that poker will ever institute a dress code, but there should at least be a rule of thumb about the number of holes a T-shirt can have or how many times it can be worn (how about once?) without being washed. At least consider "Casual Friday" as a guide, especially if you're going to be on TV.

If you are a superstitious person, you may be forced to develop your own fashion code. T. J. Cloutier develops relationships with certain shirts. "I wore a blue terrycloth dress shirt at the Bicycle the first year I won it, so I brought it back the next year, and I won it again. Then I brought it back the next year and I won it again. Then, somehow," he confesses, laughing, "it was too old to wear anymore."

OTHER ACCOUTREMENTS

Stop by the $10/20 table at Hollywood Park and more likely than not, seated to the dealer's right, will be a very large man named "Briz." You'll know it's him because, jutting just above the edge of the rail, looming behind his cards, a huge gold belt buckle—BRIZ—will be staring back at you. The message is clear. Tangle with Briz at your own risk.

Susie Isaacs, a fine poker player with a somewhat questionable sense of fashion—i.e., outfits and hats covered with pictures of playing cards—has developed her own line of "designer gaming jewelry." Whether this is a blessing or a further descent into the depths of kitsch is up to you to decide.

Some people have lucky socks. Others wear good luck medallions, New Age crystals, or enough gold jewelry to rival Mr. T. In the end, you should wear whatever makes you feel like a winner. Because in poker, it's definitely more important to feel good than to look good. As Chris Ferguson, winner of the 2000 World Series, correctly advises, "You can bring your favorite teddy bear to the table if it makes you feel lucky. Just don't blame the teddy bear if your luck turns around."

THE PRICE OF ADMISSION

Casinos are—and should be—in the business of making money. In those games that are played against "the House," the path to profitability is clear. Play roulette and, on average, you'll give back 5 percent more than you'll win. A blackjack player using "perfect strategy" can narrow the odds considerably, but will still be a moderate loser in the long run.

The poker table, however, forces the House into the far less profitable position of impartial observer. To keep the lights on and the dealers dealing, cardrooms have to take a cut from the players.

THE RAKE

While some casinos charge an hourly fee to play at their tables, most accrue their profits in the form of a rake, a small fee removed from every pot. The size of the rake can vary depending on the locale and type of game, but typically tends to be $3 to $5 per deal.

This may not seem like a lot when you're taking down a $200 pot, but the rake adds up over time. Let's say that your local cardroom deals about forty hands an hour, taking an average of $3 from every pot. That's $120 that will disappear from the table every hour. If there are eight players at your table, each of you is paying, on average, $15/hour for the privilege to play in the game.

Thus you'll often hear poker players talk about "beating the rake." To be a consistent winner in the hypothetical game described above, you not only have to be better than your opponents, but you have to be at least $15/hour better. If you're playing for pure entertainment, it's not much more expensive than a movie. But if you're a would-be rounder attempting to grind out a living, the rake can be a serious hindrance to paying the rent.

Beating the rake is an unavoidable part of the casino game. Here are a few things you should keep in mind:

- **Do the math.** Find out how much the rake is before you start playing. The rake makes some low-stakes games (i.e., $2/4 or $3/6) nearly impossible to beat unless you are absolutely dominating the competition.

- **Play fewer hands.** Yes, the table is losing money to the house, but there's no reason why you have to pay your fair share. The more pots you get involved in, the more you end up contributing to the hourly drain. Every hand you don't play is money saved. In other words, tight play becomes even more important in a raked game. Let the maniac who gets involved in every hand take the brunt of it.

- **Smaller can be better.** Cardrooms will often reduce, and in some cases even eliminate, the rake in games that are less than full. If your table suddenly becomes short-handed, ask the dealer if they'll consider a discount.

- **Play higher stakes.** A $5/pot rake at a $3/6 table seems downright oppressive, but the same rake might seem bearable at a $15/30 table, where pots are typically played for hundreds of dollars. It's generally accepted that if you're treating poker as a source of income, you have to be playing at least $10/20 to have a shot at consistently beating the rake. This is tricky advice to follow, however, as the level of competition tends to increase along with the stakes.

TIPPING

The last "hidden cost" of cardroom poker is tipping, which can be a somewhat controversial subject for some players (and most dealers!).

Those in favor say that poker dealers are part of a low-paying service industry that is a lot like waiting tables. Opponents of tipping reply with something like, "Tough nuts! They get a salary, don't they? And besides, she's been dealing me nothing but **rags** all night!"

According to a recent study, poker dealers in southern Nevada are paid an average salary of $6.12/hour, around a dollar more than the state minimum wage. This isn't very much for a job that requires a decent amount of skill (just think about how many "misdeals" take place in an average home game) and the wherewithal to remain calm while angry players pelt them with curses, insults—even cards! In other words, the question isn't whether to tip, but how much. It's ultimately a matter of personal preference, but a dollar per pot won seems to be about the norm.

While you shouldn't feel compelled to tip those dealers who are rude or incompetent, keep in mind that being on the receiving end of awful cards has absolutely nothing to do with the dealer. Really. It doesn't.

"BAD BEAT" JACKPOTS

There are few worse feelings in life (well, poker, anyway) than a bad beat. To help combat the resulting despair, many casinos have added a "bad beat jackpot"—a payout, usually in the thousands (if not tens of thousands) to the unlucky loser of a big hand versus big hand showdown. The requirements are specific to each casino, but are usually along the line of aces full getting cracked by a better aces full, four of a kind, or a straight flush.

Most of these jackpots also provide some extra financial remuneration to the already lucky winner, to everyone seated at the table and, by extension, the dealer, who can generally expect a hefty tip for demonstrating such prowess as to have dealt the hands in the first place. When a jackpot possibility arises—like three aces on the flop (giving aces full to anyone with a pocket pair)—the excitement is often palpable, the whisper "jackpot hand" speeding around the table like electricity.* When the hole cards are turned over, the players will erupt in celebration—or mutter about the one that got away.

Bad beat jackpots have a mixed reputation among poker players. Gamblers love them, as the chance to come home from a low-stakes game with ten grand aligns neatly with their reason for living. More conservative players, however, curse them, recognizing that the house is not providing this service out of some sympathy for battered players. The casino funds the jackpot by taking an extra

---

* Actually, you need to be careful what you say, even if you're whispering. Many cardrooms reserve the right to negate a bad beat jackpot if anyone actually mentions it while the hand is in play.

dollar or so (in addition to the rake) out of every pot. And just like the state lottery, the house is under no obligation to include all of this money in the actual prize pool. In other words, it's another chance for the casino to skim money from the players.

Like them or not, they do exist, and they are a lot of fun to win. They also create the phenomenon known as *bad beat jackpot odds.* Say you're up against what you're pretty sure is aces full, but you've got one card in the deck that will make you a straight flush. While the pot alone will rarely give you enough incentive to chase that card, the size of the bad beat jackpot will more likely than not give you whatever odds you need to make the call.

The casinos, of course, recognize that the existence of the jackpot encourages players to hang around with more speculative hands in the hopes of a miracle card, building bigger pots, creating larger rakes, and—you guessed it— allowing them to skim even more money off the players.

PLAYERS' REVENGE: COMPS AND CLUBS

Fortunately for the player, that old-time free market competition has its rewards. Most casinos know you can just as easily go across the street (or to an online poker site), and they have instituted all kinds of loyalty and rewards programs to keep you coming back.

Some will refund your rake if you play a certain number of hours a month. Others offer "points" that you can exchange for food, lodging, clothing (as long as you don't mind wearing clothing embroidered with the casino's logo), even travel coffee mugs and binoculars. Cardrooms will

often host lotto-style giveaways—for prizes like new cars—
or freerolls, poker tournaments without any entry fees.

Hardly the fabled free lunch, but it's as close as you're
likely to get. If you're going to play with any regularity at a
particular cardroom, the three minutes or so it takes to
sign up will be time well spent.

THE FIRST TRIP TO THE CARDROOM

Walking into a cardroom for the first time can be a pretty
intimidating experience. Poker's recent surge in popularity
has made getting a seat more difficult than dining in a four-
star restaurant (expect to wait at least an hour for a spot at the
Bellagio on a Friday night) and has created veritable mob
scenes near the door. What follows will be old hat for experienced players, but may save some aggravation for first-timers.

When you enter the poker room, your first stop will be
the **board,** where you can sign up for a table. In some
rooms, the board is literally a board; in others, it's more
like the reservation clipboard at a restaurant. Most actually take reservations if you call ahead, something to consider if you're looking to play during peak hours. Keep in
mind as well that rooms are often divided into high-limit
and low-limit sections, each with their own board.

The **host** will take your initials (or your first name and last
initial) and call you when the seat you've requested is avail-
able. Unless they happen to be your actual initials, giving
"AA" to the host is neither original nor particularly clever. If
you're planning to step outside to smoke a cigarette, use the
facilities, or sneak in a few hands of blackjack, tell the host to
"lock up your seat," which will buy you a couple of minutes if

your name gets called and you're not around to hear it. There are those times when the wait is so unbearable that you might be tempted to slip the host a discreet bribe. Sometimes it actually works; use your judgment here.

Once you are called, you'll be directed to the **floorman,** who will escort you to your seat. Floormen may be the most important people to befriend in a cardroom, as they know the flavor of every game going and are the final arbiters in all table disputes. A "friendly" floorman will direct you to the center seat at a table full of fish and take pains to see your side in any argument. Occasionally they can be counted on to help you find a seat on very crowded nights, or to reward your friendship with small perks like VIP parking. Hint: Tipping is a very good way to make friends.

After you take your seat, a chip runner will take your money and return with chips. Most players like to buy in for a **rack** (one hundred chips) of whatever denomination is in play; aggressive players will buy two. Tipping the chip runner for the buy-in isn't strictly necessary, but if you later ask him or her to "color you up"—that is, exchange your full racks of chips for a smaller number in a higher denomination—it's common courtesy to stick an extra chip into the rack. As for your physical bankroll, it's a lot more intimidating to buy into a game with hundreds peeled off a roll than it is to pull a stack of ATM-fresh twenties out of your wallet.

The **dealer** may be the most unfairly maligned profession on the planet. The upside is that years of being unfairly blamed for events far beyond the control of mere mortals has helped many of them to develop a clever, self-deprecating wit that is all their own. Whether you find a dealer to be an innocent bystander to the whims of fate or a vile spawn of some lower level of hell whose sole purpose is to separate you from your chips is a good indication of your character as a poker player.

One of the many burdens faced by these professionals is that while they will do all of the manual labor of shuffling,* passing out and collecting the cards, and regulating the betting, the title of "dealer" is actually reserved for one of the players! (Perhaps poker dealers deserve their own unique nickname, like "card mediums" or "punching bags.") This player/dealer—whose reign is commemorated by a white plastic disc called the button—gets the advantage (as discussed in Chapter Three) of being one of the last people to act during the pre-flop betting and the last person to act on every subsequent round of betting. This is the equivalent of prime real estate for poker players, who covet good position the way that some people long for an ocean view.

The button bestows its magnificent powers for only a single hand before moving, clockwise, to the next player at the table. For purposes of clarity, from here on out we'll call this person "the button," saving the term "dealer" for the person who shuffles and deals the cards.

If you're sitting down to a new game, the dealer will deal one card, face up, to each player. The player with the highest card—aces are tops, ties are broken by appealing to the suits, which are ranked, from highest to lowest, spades, hearts, diamonds, and clubs—wins the button for the inaugural deal.

If you are joining a game in progress, you are going to

---

* In some places, this task has been taken away from the dealers by automated shuffling machines. It's not a move meant to stem cheating; rather the intention is to speed up play—the more hands that are dealt, the more rakes the House can collect.

have to **post a blind** before you can participate in a hand. While you can post a blind from any position except the button, most players will wait until it's their turn to be the big blind (a bet that they would have had to make anyway) or the button has made its way to the player on their immediate left (ensuring that this forced bet can at least benefit from the best possible position). Posting a blind from anywhere else generally marks a player as a rube or someone too impatient to wait the five minutes or so for a better spot to get involved in the action—in other words, the kind of person who causes experienced players to salivate.

"BURN AND TURN"

Watch a professional poker dealer, and you'll see her "burn" the top card in the deck, throwing it face down into the muck, before dealing the flop, turn, and river.

It's not just a quirky habit, but a longstanding measure to discourage cheating. An unscrupulous card marker might be able to deduce the identity of the "burn" card before it's dealt, but the actual "turn" card remains safely hidden from view.

While you're unlikely to encounter marked cards in a casino, it's nice to know that you're being protected.

THE CARDROOM BILL OF RIGHTS

There are a good many idiosyncrasies in casino poker that may differ from your home game. Failure to understand them may result in some expensive mistakes and/or penalties, so know your rights!

THE RIGHT TO PROTECT YOUR CARDS

Dealers are under a lot of pressure to deal as many hands as they can. As a result, they will sometimes mistakenly sweep a "live" hand into the **muck,** the black hole of the poker table. You can complain all you want to the floorman, but once your cards touch any of the other cards in the muck, they are, without ifs, ands, or buts, dead.

As a poker player, however, you do have the right to protect your hole cards by placing something on top of them. Most players use a chip. More creative or superstitious types, however, have been known to protect their cards with all kinds of talismans, statuettes, lucky crystals, etc.

Just remember that while abstinence may be the best way to avoid losing money, if you do decide to play, use protection.

THE RIGHT TO A NEW DECK

During the course of play, dealers are regularly supplied with new "setups," poker talk for two brand-new decks of cards. If you don't like the deck that's in play, you have the right to ask the dealer to use the other one. If the other one has already been used, you can ask for a new setup.

It's a rule that once made a lot of sense before the advent of professional dealers (yes, players used to deal their own hands) and security cameras. Now it's mainly used by superstitious players who don't like the way their luck is running. Players who aren't as superstitious mainly get annoyed by these requests. When a dealer gets a new setup, he or she has to spread both decks out on the table, examining each to insure that all of the cards are there, before shuffling and dealing can resume. It's a time-consuming business. In an attempt to mitigate the willy-nilly abuse of this rule, most rooms will make you wait until a new deck has made a full orbit around the table before you can request another one.

THE RIGHT TO A NEW SEAT

When, during the course of a game, a seat opens up at your table, you have the right to move to it. Depending on the position of the button, you may be forced to re-post one or both of the blinds.

While this is an action usually inspired by a superstitious belief in "hot" or "cold" seats, there are sometimes some very good reasons for moving. When there's a maniac at the table, experienced players will usually want to sit directly to their left (where they can raise the maniac's reckless bets in an attempt to drive out the rest of the field with a double-bet) or to their right (where they can see how everyone else at the table responds to the maniac's action before deciding on their own course). It's also a good way to get away from people whose smoking, body odor, or incessant chatter is starting to get to you.

THE RIGHT TO LOOK AT ANOTHER PLAYER'S CARDS

You have the right to ask to see any hand that, once play has ended, hasn't been folded. It's considered bad form, however, to make such requests with any regularity— allowing your opponents to lose with dignity isn't just common courtesy, it's good poker.

There's also nothing illegal about sneaking a peek if the person sitting next to you is careless in the way he or she looks at her cards, a trait especially common among the very elderly and the very drunk. A good rule of thumb if someone is repeatedly exposing his hole cards to you is to offer up a single warning. After that it's fair game.

SOME RIGHTS THAT YOU DON'T HAVE
THE RIGHT TO SPLASH THE POT

You'll recall the climactic showdown in *Rounders,* where Teddy KGB makes a bet by tossing a handful of chips into the center of the table. Mike McDermott, his opponent, asks him to stop "splashing the pot." To which Teddy replies, "It's my club, and I can splash the pot any time I damn well please."

In most cardrooms, however, you cannot splash the pot any time you damn well please, or ever, for that matter, as it's very difficult to discern exactly how much money is being tossed in there. When you're looking to add chips to the pot, just place them in front of you, allowing the dealer to verify the size of the bet before sweeping them into the middle.

THE RIGHT TO STRING BET

A devious poker player will do whatever possible to extract information from his or her fellow players. One way of doing this is to call a bet, take a quick look around the table to see how people react, then reach back into his or her stack to pull out a raise.

This is called a **string bet,** and it's illegal in almost every cardroom. If you want to raise, you need to do it in one distinct action. You can also say "raise" (hopefully in a voice that exudes confidence in your hand) before pushing any of your chips forward, giving you free license to go back and forth to your stack at will before committing to an amount.

THE RIGHT TO ANNOUNCE YOUR HAND

In a recent World Poker Tour event, Paul "Dot.com" Phillips faced an all-in raise from his sole opponent, Mel Judah. Attempting to extract some clue to the nature of Judah's hand, Phillips announced his own: "I've got a straight, Mel."

While Phillips's action went unpunished in the moment it occurred, commentator Mike Sexton correctly pointed out that what he had done was a violation of tournament rules. You aren't allowed to reveal your hand, whether verbally or physically, while it's in play.

CHEATING

In the mid-1970s, four California draw poker players became quite proficient at duping their opponents at the $30/60 table out of a little extra money. It went a little something like this:

Mr. Grey (not his real name, of course) looks down at his

cards to find three aces, a huge starting hand in draw poker. He fans his cards, slightly repositioning his thumb, and opens with a $30 raise.*

Unaware of the web of deceit surrounding them, a couple of unlucky players call. The action gets to Mr. Pink, who, having picked up on Mr. Grey's subtle signal, reraises to $60 with whatever junk cards he happens to be holding. A third player, Mr. Yellow, calls the $60 cold. Mr. Grey merely calls the raise, trapping the two pigeons in the middle into calling the second bet.

After the draw, Mr. Grey opens with a bet. The two pigeons call, as does Mr. Pink. Mr. Yellow, however, raises. Mr. Grey calls, the two pigeons call . . . and Mr. Pink raises.

Not only are the two pigeons likely to lose to Mr. Grey's powerhouse hand, but it's going to cost them several extra bets to do so.

Lest the other players at the table get suspicious, Mr. Grey bids his farewell, only to be replaced by Mr. Orange, the fourth co-conspirator, who starts the process all over again.

This colorful team wasn't the only group working this sort of angle. Mr. Grey recalls a time when, intending to play a more legitimate style of poker, he took his seat in a nine-person game. Before he could play his first hand, he was tapped on the shoulder by the floorman, an old friend of his, who invited him to come see the cardroom's new state-of-the-art security system. As they ventured into the privacy of a backroom, the floorman explained that the eight other people at the table were *all* in cahoots, waiting for an unlucky ninth to join their game.

---

* In this style of California draw, the first player into the pot was obligated to open with a raise.

Needless to say, Mr. Grey found another table. What's troubling about this story is that the floorman—and by extension, the cardroom—not only knew about the cheating, but did nothing to prevent it. In their eyes, action was action, and far be it for them to interfere.

Fortunately, the golden age of cheating has come to an end. After one of these Gardena cardrooms was forced to shut its doors—its notoriety as a haven for cheaters had become so prevalent that the "action" simply stopped coming—the surviving casinos began to realize that they could no longer turn a blind eye to their reputations. Most of today's rooms have "eyes in the sky" and scrupulous floormen who are on the lookout for this kind of activity. You should feel very secure about playing in public cardrooms that are well regulated—the chances that you will be cheated are very, very small. That being said, should you suspect any funny business, get up from the game and find another, discreetly notifying the floorman en route.

OTHER CARDROOM QUIRKS

Nowadays, the rules of hold'em are pretty well etched in stone. Each cardroom, however, has its own idiosyncrasies that you should be aware of.

CAPPED POTS

Most cardrooms limit the number of raises that can be made on any particular street, usually to three (allowing a total of four bets), sometimes four (or five bets total) before the betting is declared capped.

Many rooms dismiss the cap when two players get

heads-up, allowing them to raise and re-raise one another until someone runs out of chips. You can ask the dealer or floorman to explain any rules particular to the table where you're seated.

KILL POTS

Revenge is sweet, an idea that's not lost on some casinos, who use **kill pots** to spice up their games. A player who wins two hands in a row gets the "kill button" and is required to post a bet—usually twice the size of the blind—on the next hand, ostensibly giving everyone else a chance to win some of their money back in a raised pot.

Many opposing players will try to take advantage of the situation by raising, getting three bets into the pot against the guy with the kill button, who has been forced to cough up the double bet with whatever random two cards he's been dealt. What's intriguing, however, is that the player with the kill button is almost always getting decent enough odds to call the raise, setting the stage for another potentially infuriating beat.

STRADDLE RAISES

Every once in a while you'll come across a player who, while sitting under the gun (the seat just to the left of the big blind, whose job it is to open the initial round of betting), likes to post a double-bet before the cards are dealt. By making a **straddle raise,** the player is committing himself—and anyone else who wants to gamble with him—to a raised pot before he's even looked at his cards. It's rarely a very profitable play. Not only are you playing a hand that, more often than not, will be less than premium, but you're committing to playing it from one of the least advantageous positions at the table. But making a straddle raise but can be an extremely effective tool if you're looking to propagate a loose table image or deliver an agonizing bad beat.

THE BEST CARDROOMS IN THE WORLD

BELLAGIO, LAS VEGAS, NEVADA

It's not the largest, but it may be the classiest poker room in the world. On any given night, you're bound to find luminaries like Doyle Brunson, Jen Harman, or Phil Ivey playing in the top section.

COMMERCE CASINO, CITY OF COMMERCE, CALIFORNIA

If poker had a heaven, it might look something like the Commerce Casino. There are more games being spread here, encompassing the full spectrum of limits, than anywhere else in the world.

FOXWOODS, MASHANTUCKET, CONNECTICUT

The Commerce of the East, the poker room at Foxwoods can hold up to seventy-six separate games at any time.

HONORABLE MENTIONS

AVIATION CLUB DE FRANCE,
PARIS, FRANCE

BAY 101, SAN JOSE, CALIFORNIA

CASINO RAY, HELSINKI, FINLAND

CONCORD CARD CASINO,
VIENNA, AUSTRIA

GROSVENOR VICTORIA CASINO,
LONDON, ENGLAND

HOLLYWOOD PARK CASINO,
INGLEWOOD, CALIFORNIA

TAJ MAHAL, ATLANTIC CITY, NEW JERSEY

INTERMISSION: HOW TO PUT A TABLE ON TILT

Winning a small pot feels good. Winning a huge pot feels great.

Sometimes you'll be lucky enough to sit at a loose table, where maniacs will raise and re-raise your nut hands all the way to the river, spoon-feeding you pot after pot.

Other times you'll find yourself at table full of tight-fisted rocks, folding too early and too often for you to realize anything but the most marginal profits. That is, unless you can transform these models of rational judgment and sober restraint into bloodthirsty, raving lunatics yelling "Cappuccino!" as they toss in their fourth bets.

The easiest way to accomplish this is to put your opponents *on tilt*, exasperating them into committing completely irrational acts, which you then exploit mercilessly.

The following strategies should be wielded with great care. Used properly, they can result in some of your most legendary winning nights. But be warned: Should you try any of these techniques and fail, you will probably look like, well, a complete ass.

DELIVER A BAD BEAT

If you're playing poker "correctly"—that is, calling or betting only when you have the right odds—you're going to suffer more bad beats than you inflict. The theory of **implied tilt odds** (or ITO), however, suggests that the correct way is not always the best way. ITO relies on the notion that calling a bet when you have no mathematical business doing so, then winning the hand, will leave your stunned opponent muttering obscenities and chasing his money for the rest of the night.

Here's an example: A super-tight player has raised and re-raised with what you (and everyone else at the table) *know* are pocket aces, after you've inexplicably raised from the small blind with 7-2s. The flop comes down A-K-2 with one of your suit. Should you continue with the hand? Odds calculated in the traditional way would say no. The implied tilt odds, however, tell you to go right ahead. Sure, you probably won't make that **runner-runner flush**, or catch running deuces to make quads against his aces full. But those few times that you do will completely destroy your opponent's faith in the natural order of the universe, and should earn you enough angry money over the rest of the session to make this a profitable play.

FEIGN DRUNKENNESS

Nobody likes a drunk. A winning drunk is even worse. Scooping big pots while seemingly intoxicated to the point of near-collapse is a sure way to piss off your opponents.

Order a drink. Say "another drink" even if it's your first. Spill a little on your lap — never underestimate the sense of smell — and alternate between holding your head miserably in your hands and erupting in fits of delirious, high-pitched giggles.

This style of play is not recommended if you actually *are* drunk, in which case you should probably tighten up your play considerably, or, better yet, sleep it off. If you're of that rare breed who actually plays *better* drunk, congratulations! You've got a natural edge.

BECOME A BULLY

Admit it. There have been times when you were pushed around by somebody stronger, smarter, or just meaner than you. Remember how you felt? Now imagine trying to play poker in that state.

Choose an opponent to pick on. Men with recently loosened ties are often your best bet, but you should select your target according to your ability to annoy certain personality types. Taunt them at every opportunity, mixing emotional torture ("Wow, that one had to hurt") with observational humor ("When did you decide to get the hair plugs?").

Then wait for an opportunity to "lie" about your hand. For example, when you're pretty sure your target has something like two pair, offer a warning like, "Don't call, I've got a flush!" When they make the crying call, turn over your full house. You will see the steam coming out of their ears.*

Bullying doesn't work on everyone, but when you find someone who gets easily offended at the poker table, it can be your best (and most perversely satisfying) weapon.

"SLOWROLLING"

Taking an unnecessarily long time to announce, analyze, or otherwise evaluate your opponent's second-best hand before turning over your winning cards—or, as they say, "slowrolling"—is a great way to make enemies at the table. This play is especially effective against old crocodiles who already resent you for being such a moronic young whippersnapper.

UNLEASH YOUR INNER ANNOYING SELF

For some, the ability to fill the air with incessant, meaningless chatter comes naturally. For others, it's an acquired skill. If you have it, nurture it. If you don't, start studying the behavioral patterns of annoying people. A distracted player is a losing player, and you want to provide as much distraction as possible.

Talk about your troubles with your girlfriend. Or your boyfriend. Or your girlfriend's boyfriend. Bemoan life

---

* Yes, revealing your hand is illegal, but there's technically nothing to prevent you from *lying* about your hole cards.

with your stepkids (real or imagined). Comment on your every move: "I guess I just have to call." Hum. Develop facial tics. Pass gas.

The trick is to create a general aura of annoyance without getting people so aggravated that they leave the table.

PRESTO!

A variant of the bad beat, wielding the power of Presto is a skill that takes a moment to learn and a lifetime to master. All you have to do is win a hold'em hand with pocket fives, declaring "Presto!" as you turn over your cards.* One's level of Presto expertise is determined by just how bad a beat gets delivered, i.e., flopping a set of fives against pocket aces is good, but gut-shotting a straight on the river represents the work of a true Presto master.

An added benefit: Once you've introduced Presto to a table, some if not all of your opponents are going to join in, creating a lot of "dumb" money.

STUDY ASIAN HISTORY

An old Chinese proverb describes a little gambling as "soothing and relaxing." Gambling has been a respectable part of Asian life since early history, so it's no surprise that the region has produced a rich cultural tradition of delivering bad beats with unique style and panache. Whether it's phrases like "Cha Ching!" and "Ai-yah!" or more physical expressions like karate chopping the table and standing up on a chair, many of the Asian greats have an uncanny ability to put their opponents on tilt. Study them carefully.

---

* It's customary to acknowledge another player's successful Presto by responding with your own cry of "Irwin!"

THE TILTBOYS

In the mid-1990s, a group of friends gathered around the shared principle of "angling"—pulling fast ones on other people and, as often as possible, on each other—in the hopes of pushing them over the edge of rational behavior. The "Tiltboys," as we called ourselves, took frequent trips to Las Vegas, Reno, San Bruno, or any other place where we could find a poker game and a steady stream of opportunities to place side bets on everything from the over/under on the total hours we'd sleep to the number of times I'd be rejected while trying to flirt with a woman at the table.

Getting angled by a fellow Tiltboy, whether by a "schneiding" on the river or a tough loss at golf, Roshambo, or the "Circle Game," would cause your level of anger—measured on the Tiltmeter—to rise, a condition that could only be cured by a successful angling of your own.

The only thing more fun than driving a fellow Tiltboy to a full head of steam might have been the opportunities to put complete strangers on megatilt. Like the time Dave "Dice Boy" Lambert—also nicknamed "Six Sigma Man" for his propensity to luck out far more often than what any statistician could conceivably describe as normal—inflicted a series of ridiculously bad beats on *Cardplayer* magazine columnist Roy Cooke at a $20/40 table. Or when we "skirted" the rules of a women's only tournament at Bay 101 by appearing in drag. (Transformed Tiltgirl Michael "Michelle" Stern took down a share of first place!)

If any of this seems intriguing, or if you're just a fan of really immature male behavior, several essays chronicling the exploits of the Tiltboys—including rare photos of "Phyllis" Gordon in a light magenta frock and a blue straw hat with a white chiffon ribbon—can be found at www.tiltboys.com.

YOUR DEFINING MOMENT

It's Wednesday afternoon, about one P.M., and your boss pokes his head into your cubicle to tell you that he's got a business meeting that will keep him out of the office for the rest of the afternoon. Ten minutes after he leaves, you're on your way to the local cardroom for some $15/$30 hold'em.

No names on the sign-up list, so you walk directly to the table, where an open seat is waiting for you. You pull $500 from your wallet, call for the chip runner, and . . . oops. There's your boss, sitting on your right.

He gives you a little smirk. "I didn't get the memo. Were you invited to this meeting?" You both have a good laugh.

But the laughs are over when, a few hands later, your boss raises to $30 from under the gun. You look down to find K♠ Q♠. Quickly scanning the table, you notice that the woman in the small blind has already peeked at her cards and seems very interested in the action.

Are you going to three-bet your boss or **smooth call** his raise and see the flop?

Well, job security is certainly an issue. But business is business—this is poker. You really want to play this hand heads-up, in position. That means eliminating the woman in the small blind.

You three-bet. The small blind pauses, thinks, then reluctantly calls. So much for isolating your boss, who, of course, calls the bet as well. Three-way action, with $150 in the pot.

The flop comes down, 10♣ 9♠ 4♦. The small blind checks, your boss bets $15.

Your play, your Defining Moment.

♥ ♦ ♣ ♠ ♥ ♦ ♣ ♠ ♥ ♦ ♣ ♠ ♥ ♦ ♣ ♠ ♥ ♦ ♣ ♠ ♥ ♦ ♣ ♠

THE ANSWER

There is now $165 in the pot. With four jacks left in the deck—or so you hope—and forty-seven cards unknown, you have about a 1 in 12 chance of turning a jack. The pot is giving you 11-to-1 odds, so clearly you must play. Instead of just calling, however, you decide that the better play—not for your career, but for the pot—is to raise. You'll almost certainly force the small blind to (finally) fold, and in all likelihood you'll get a "free" look at the turn card.

You raise. The small blind folds and your boss calls. You figure him for A-10.

The turn brings the 5♥ ♥. Your boss checks. Your plan is working, and there's no reason to deviate from it now. There is no way your boss can fold a pair at this point, so you check and take your "free" shot at the river.

B-I-N-G-O! The river brings the J♥. Your boss fires $30 at the pot. But you have the immortal nuts. You're the boss now, and the boss has to raise. He makes the crying call, you scoop the pot.

"Gotta run, folks. Business meeting in a few minutes," he says as he rises from the table. "Can we expect to see you back at work today?"

"I am at work," you retort, and go about stacking his chips.

DAVID YELLEN

Phil Gordon is a world-class poker player, respected teacher, and the author of *Phil Gordon's Little Green Book* and *Phil Gordon's Little Blue Book*. He has won more than $2.3 million in tournament purses, including two wins on the *World Poker Tour* and five final table appearances at the *World Series of Poker* championship event. He lives in Las Vegas.

For more advanced instruction, see *Phil Gordon's Little Green Book*—a thorough analysis of all strategic concepts in No Limit Texas Hold'em.

For a practical look at hands with complete, professional analysis, get *Phil Gordon's Little Blue Book*—75 hands of No Limit Hold'em from cash games, the tournament trail, and from the internet.

If you'd like to play poker with Phil, you can find him playing exclusively at FullTiltPoker.com along with some of the best players in the game: Phil Ivey, Chris Ferguson, Howard Lederer, John Juanda, Erick Lindgren, Andy Bloch, Jennifer Harman, Gus Hansen, Erik Seidel, and more.